Your
Horoscope
2021

....

Gemini

22 May – 21 June

igloobooks

igloobooks

Published in 2020
by Igloo Books Ltd
Cottage Farm
Sywell
NN6 0BJ
www.igloobooks.com

0820 001
2 4 6 8 10 9 7 5 3 1
ISBN 978-1-83852-318-3

Written by Belinda Campbell and Denise Evans

Cover design by Simon Parker
Edited by Bobby Newlyn-Jones

Printed and manufactured in China

CONTENTS

....

INTRODUCTION
. . . .

This 15-month guide has been designed and written to give a concise and accessible insight into both the nature of your star sign and the year ahead. Divided into two main sections, the first section of this guide will give you an overview of your character in order to help you understand how you think, perceive the world and interact with others and – perhaps just as importantly – why. You'll soon see that your zodiac sign is not just affected by a few stars in the sky, but by planets, elements, and a whole host of other factors, too.

The second section of this guide is made up of daily forecasts. Use these to increase your awareness of what might appear on your horizon so that you're better equipped to deal with the days ahead. While this should never be used to dictate your life, it can be useful to see how your energies might be affected or influenced, which in turn can help you prepare for what life might throw your way.

By the end of these 15 months, these two sections should have given you a deeper understanding and awareness of yourself and, in turn, the world around you. There are never any definite certainties, but with an open mind you will find guidance for what might be, and learn to take more control of your own destiny.

THE CHARACTER OF THE TWINS

· · · · · · · · · · · · · · · · · · ·

Expect a triple dose of conversation, charisma and intellect from Geminians. Not usually satisfied with focusing on one thing at a time, these artful communicators will likely be Tweeting celebrities, texting colleagues and Snapchatting friends simultaneously without even breaking a sweat. Fortunately, they often have twice as much energy as everyone else, so won't usually have an issue keeping up with their active social lives. Lively and affable, Geminians are friends, or at least acquainted, with everyone around them. Frequently found fluttering from friend to friend, these social butterflies touch the lives of many.

Geminians crave constant mental stimulation, which is perhaps why they are well known for being intelligent. They are expert conversationalists and are formidable opponents in a debate. Yet, as much as Geminians are happy to lead or even dominate a conversation, they are also just as eager to listen. To satisfy their eternal curiosity, they can be keen on learning all the facts about a story that has captured their interest, be it serious news or the latest celebrity break-up. This love for knowledge can lead to Geminians learning many secrets, but their athletic approach to conversing could result in them running around and sharing what they've learnt with everyone else. They would be wise to keep any gossiping to a minimum and perhaps apply their knack for narrative to writing, like fellow Geminians Arthur Conan Doyle and Salman Rushdie.

THE TWINS

Double the trouble or twice the fun? The Twins that represent
Gemini can be an indication of many, and sometimes
Opposing, traits. Castor and Pollux were twin half-brothers
from Greek mythology that have commonly been portrayed
as the Gemini symbol. In some stories, Castor is thought to
be mortal, while Pollux is immortal. When Castor dies, he
is sent to the Underworld ruled by Hades, leaving Pollux in
Olympus with the Gods. The light and dark of this tale is a
perfect example of the two sides that many Geminians are
commonly thought to display. Their moods are changeable,
which can make them seem deceitful or two-faced, while their
Mutable quality makes them advocates of change. Whether it's
changing their hair colour or even their postcode, these fluid
beings are often unrecognisable from one day to the next.
However, Geminians are fascinating characters to try and get
to know.

MERCURY

Orbiting the Sun faster than any other planet in the Solar System, travel and speed are two associations that Geminians surely inherit from their ruling planet of Mercury. Named after the Roman god of communication, trickery and travel, winged Mercury is a perfect embodiment of Air sign Gemini. The speed in which we travel and communicate is ever increasing, much to the joy of quick-thinking Geminians. Feeling the influence of Mercury, they favour instantly gratifying forms of interaction. However, texting, Tweeting and talking rapidly can mean that Geminians may not always think before they speak or press send. 'Mercury in retrograde' is a phrase that is often met with fearful faces, but what does it mean? Three times a year, Mercury seemingly begins to move backwards and is blamed for many communication, media, technology and travel failures. Remember when Geminian Kanye West interrupted Taylor Swift's 2009 MTV Video Music Award Speech? That was during a Mercury retrograde!

ELEMENTS, MODES AND POLARITIES

Each sign is made up of a unique combination of three defining groups: elements, modes and polarities. Each of these defining parts can manifest themselves in good and bad ways, and none should be seen as a positive or a negative – including the polarities! Just like a jigsaw puzzle, piecing these groups together can help illuminate why each sign has certain characteristics and help us find a balance.

ELEMENTS

Fire: Dynamic and adventurous, signs with Fire in them can be extroverted. Others are naturally drawn to them because of the positive light they give off, as well as their high levels of energy and confidence.

Earth: Signs with the Earth element are steady and driven with their ambitions. They make for a solid friend, parent or partner due to their grounded influence and nurturing nature.

Air: The invisible element that influences each of the other elements significantly, Air signs will provide much-needed perspective to others with their fair thinking, verbal skills and key ideas.

Water: Warm in the shallows and freezing as ice. This mysterious element is essential to the growth of everything around it, through its emotional depth and empathy.

MODES

Cardinal: Pioneers of the calendar, cardinal signs jump-start each season and are the energetic go-getters.

Fixed: Marking the middle of the calendar, fixed signs firmly denote and value steadiness and reliability.

Mutable: As the seasons end, the mutable signs adapt and give themselves over gladly to the promise of change.

POLARITIES

Positive: Typically extroverted, positive signs take physical action and embrace outside stimulus in their life.

Negative: Usually introverted, negative signs value emotional development and experiencing life from the inside out.

GEMINI IN BRIEF

The table below shows the key attributes of Geminians. Use it for quick reference and to understand more about this fascinating sign.

SYMBOL	RULING PLANET	MODE	ELEMENT	HOUSE
The Twins	Mercury	Mutable	Air	Third

COLOUR	BODY PART	POLARITY	GENDER	POLAR SIGN
Yellow, Blue	Shoulders, Arms, Hands, Nervous System	Positive	Masculine	Sagittarius

ROMANTIC
RELATIONSHIPS
· · · · · · · · · · · · · · · · ·

Like their element of Air, Geminians have a lightness to them that lifts others up. However, anyone who falls for these flyaway characters will need to work hard to keep their interests piqued. Geminians can reach dizzying heights of ecstasy in love but soon lose their curiosity, leaving partners plummeting back to Earth painfully. They are likely to have several possible love interests simultaneously, on multiple different dating apps, but may be quick to swipe left or abandon conversations if they get bored. Speed dating could be an interesting night out for this fast-paced chatterbox!

With a love of change and speed, Geminians may walk away from relationships too quickly. To hold onto a relationship, they will need to slow down and take a moment to honestly discuss whatever issues need to be mended. Nothing is perfect, and the most worthwhile endeavours are usually those that take time and effort – something that Geminians would do well to consider in their love lives. Whilst they are expert communicators, taking the time to pause and reflect on problems in a relationship will probably not come easily, and will be something they need to work hard at.

Not ones to take themselves too seriously, Geminians will appreciate energetic lovers that they can have fun with. Thanks to their Mutable quality, they can be very easy-going in relationships and are unlikely to fight for the reigns of control. They usually value partners who are similarly relaxed, but also could be attracted to more-forthright types who take the lead and encourage them to explore new heights. Keep curious Geminians intrigued and their love will be invigorating.

ARIES: COMPATIBILITY 4/5

Though very different in their approaches to relationships, these two Positive signs can bring out the very best in one another. Communication is key for any relationship, and the Geminian's talkative nature can help the Arian to vocalise dreams and ideas. These two can form an intellectual bond that lays a strong foundation for love. The Twins and Ram are both guilty of starting projects and not finishing them, which can extend to their relationship with each other. However, their similarities and positive natures are likely to still see them part as friends if the romance extinguishes.

TAURUS: COMPATIBILITY 2/5

Three may prove to be a crowd. The duality of a Geminian, characterised in the Twin symbol, can make a Taurean feel uneasy about starting a romantic relationship. The Earth sign of Taurus mixed with airy Gemini may not be an easy joining, but if the Taurean can budge on set ideas then love could grow happily here. The Geminian's good communication skills help when understanding the Taurean's needs, providing the love and security that is craved. Communication, trust and flexibility should be this couple's mantra if they are to go the distance.

GEMINI: COMPATIBILITY 4/5

A Geminian couple is likely to be a roaring hit at social gatherings. This pair can share late-night stimulating conversations until the early hours of the morning, and probably still be energised enough to make that brunch date. Life might feel like a constant party when two Geminians unite, but they may struggle to connect deeply on an emotional level. These smart thinkers match each other in many compatible ways, so this relationship will surely be full of shared thoughts and exciting adventures.

CANCER: COMPATIBILITY 2/5

This Air and Water pairing can feel too far apart personality-wise to make a good match, but the differences could actually prove to be strengthening. The Geminian is led by the mind and the Cancerian by emotion. These contrasting perspectives can lead to misunderstandings and arguments if the line of communication isn't clear. The Geminian can help the Cancerian communicate thoughts and feelings aloud rather than keeping them bottled up, while the Cancerian can provide lessons on the value of sensitivity. With so much to learn from one another, understanding and acceptance is vital to their success.

LEO: COMPATIBILITY 4/5

The inner Leonian child can be just what the youthful sign of Gemini asked for. This love can be like a children's story full of love and adventure, think Peter Pan and Wendy. The high-energy Leonian was born to lead, whilst the Mutable Geminian is happy to take this Lion's hand and fly speedily off to Neverland! The Leonian will encourage the Geminian to take an active part in the important choices in their lives. Both Positive signs, their extrovert energies and curious natures will see this Air and Fire match embarking on endless adventures.

VIRGO: COMPATIBILITY 1/5

A Virgoan may initially be attracted to a Geminian's charm and wit, but is likely to soon feel irritated by the flights of fancy. The steady Virgoan can feel too reserved for the Geminian, and the fast-paced Geminian can be too unpredictable for the Virgoan. Both ruled by Mercury and strong believers in communication, these otherwise contrasting characters may end up feeling as if they are speaking two completely different languages. However, their mutual love of change and talent for adaptability may well be what makes this relationship last longer than predicted.

LIBRA: COMPATIBILITY 3/5

With Libra ruled by the planet of love, Venus, and Gemini by the planet of communication, Mercury, this partnership should be founded on affection and understanding. The debate-loving Geminian and peace-seeking Libran will likely have their conflicts. If love troubles do arise, these two will have a good chance of having the verbal skills and creative thinking to work out their issues. Both can have trouble making up their minds, however. The Libran's Cardinal instinct usually sets in to help make the course of action clear, much to the delight of the Mutable Geminian.

SCORPIO: COMPATIBILITY 3/5

Passionate debates are definitely on the menu for a Scorpian and Geminian in love. The Scorpian's Water element will bring emotional depth to the relationship, whilst the Geminian's Air influence will help breathe a fresh perspective on things. The Scorpian risks suffocating the Geminian with intense emotions if turned toxic. The Geminian can be flirtatious, which can trigger the Scorpian's jealousy, but the Geminian isn't scared of arguing, and actually quite likes the stimulation. Being Fixed, the Scorpian values steadiness so may find the flighty Geminian too unreliable. However, this relationship has the potential to be full of spice and interest.

SAGITTARIUS: COMPATIBILITY 5/5

'I love you just the way you are' could be the vows of a strongly independent Sagittarian and Geminian. Despite both being Mutable and willing to adapt, there is unlikely to be anything about this match that either partner will want to change about the other. Being opposite on the zodiac calendar, the love between the Sagittarian and Geminian is usually always going to be unique. For the easily bored Geminian, the adventurous Sagittarian is a perfect fit, ensuring that this couple has endless days of love and fun ahead.

CAPRICORN: COMPATIBILITY 1/5

This Earth and Air coupling may be an unlikely match, but an awareness of the differences could help create a stronger bond. The Capricornian appreciates the tangible, a good career and beautiful home, whilst the Geminian loves exciting ideas and the invisible workings of the mind. Whilst the Geminian's Mutable element fits well with the Capricornian's Cardinal aspect, what drives the Capricornian may be at odds with the Geminian. This polar-opposite couple – the Capricornian Negative and the Geminian Positive – may struggle to find common ground, but could stand to learn the most.

AQUARIUS: COMPATIBILITY 4/5

An individualist Aquarian and dual-personality Geminian can make for a compatible trio. Born in the eleventh house that signifies community and friendship, the Aquarian thrives in groups and will be a fantastic partner to the social butterfly Geminian. Mutable in nature, the Geminian is happy to follow the Aquarian's Fixed lead, which will likely bring a steadiness to the relationship. Both share the element of Air and are Positive, so are likely to have lots in common. With the Geminian's love of change and the Aquarian's need for progress, these two could create a bright and revolutionary future together.

PISCES: COMPATIBILITY 3/5

As fluid as water and as free flowing as air, a Piscean and Geminian can experience an extremely flexible and forgiving relationship if they fall for one another. Both Mutable, this couple is highly compatible and will not fight for leadership, but rather rule side by side. Whilst these two may not always perfectly understand each other, their open-minded attitudes will help resolve any disagreements. Whilst the Geminian is led by the mind-influence of Mercury, contrastingly, the Piscean's influence of Water means that they can both be ruled by their emotions. A meeting of the head and heart will be key.

FAMILY AND FRIENDS

. . . .

'You think you know someone, and then you find out they're a Geminian'. That's the sentiment friends and family of Geminians may express. To truly know Geminians is to be able to identify their light and dark sides, their love of gossip and their passion for politics. Geminians should try to get to know both sides of themselves, just as much as their friends and family should. Their duality means they can be extremely good at acting as go-betweens to friends and families. Able to see two sides to every story, Geminians can act a bridge of communication between two contrasting sides, making them potential peacemakers. Although they may instigate debates that turn into arguments, their knack for seeing multiple perspectives makes them a voice of reason that shouldn't be ignored.

Whether it's about global warming, last night's game or the glass of wine in their hand, Geminians will have an opinion and debate it to the death. Not in it just to win to it, they have endless curiosity and enjoy being tested as it satisfies their love of learning. Rather than shy away from friends or family who challenge their intellect, stimulating relationships are ones that Geminians will usually try harder to hold on to. Be sure to bring the sparkliest conversation to one of their infamous dinner parties. However, if they fail to be entertained then they will move swiftly on, abandoning a dull conversation and searching quickly for something of more interest elsewhere. Geminians do not attempt to conceal their dwindling interest, so anyone wishing to hold their attention should watch closely – and be ready to change the subject!

Being related to Geminians, who carry the element of Air, can sometimes feel like being caught up in a gale-force wind. Those closest will see them at their stormiest and strongest. Perhaps the quote often attributed to Geminian Marilyn Monroe best summed it up: "If you can't handle me at my worst, then you sure as hell don't deserve me at my best". Geminians talk non-stop and with endless energy, but if friends and family aren't left exhausted they will no doubt feel enlivened. Their need for constant change, even in relationships, may mean that the dynamics between family and friends constantly evolves and changes too. Having the energy to keep up with Geminians mentally will be a task and a half, but can have exciting rewards. The young energy of Leonians makes them perfect playmates, whilst fellow Geminians are sure to make for more fun.

MONEY AND CAREERS

· · · · · · · · · · · · · · · · ·

Being a particular star sign will not dictate certain types of career, but it can help identify potential areas for thriving in. Conversely, to succeed in the workplace, it is just as important to understand strengths and weaknesses to achieve career and financial goals.

The planet Mercury is thought to be able to change the way that people think, just like the influential Geminians who are ruled by it. These charismatic characters have a silver tongue and are more than capable of imprinting their intellect and ideas on those they encounter. They will likely have an aptitude for sales, but sometimes what they sell best is themselves. Kings, queens, prime ministers and presidents, Geminians have been ruling the world for decades. U.S. President Donald Trump is just one of the latest in a long line of influential Geminians to make a mark in politics. Strategy, intellect, communication and creating change are all defining features of Geminians and successful leaders. They have a great ability to multitask, so are usually best suited to a career that challenges them intellectually. Therefore, a career in politics is a strong potential avenue.

The youth associated with Mercury gives Geminians an eternal vitality, but could also mean that they are prone to making blunders. Fortunately, they love learning, so will usually grow from their mistakes. A teaching environment could be well suited to Geminians. Their ability to communicate and their influential way of thinking could make them favoured teachers amongst pupils. The annual changeover of students would also be a bonus for Mutable Geminians, as long as the lessons themselves aren't too repetitive. They can become bored easily, so will not happily remain in a job that stays the same or prevents them from evolving in some way. Their love of words and narrative could mean that writing is where their talents best bloom, as with Geminian Salman Rushdie.

As with family, colleagues cannot be chosen. Therefore, it can be advantageous to use star signs to learn about their key characteristics and discover the best ways of working together. With the same element of Air, Librans and Aquarians will connect with Geminians on a thoughtful level, and can make inspiring and influential colleagues. Geminian Paul McCartney and Libran John Lennon are a great example of the dizzying heights of success that these two deep-thinkers can help each other reach. Steady Taureans are likely to lock horns with flighty Geminians over their advocacy for change in a work environment. An extra dollop of patience and understanding should be served up if they find themselves on the same team.

HEALTH AND WELLBEING

· · · · · · · · · · · · · · · · · ·

Moved by their element Air, Geminians are full of ideas
and insights that will usually be heard loud and clear
thanks to their influence of Mercury, the planet signifying
communication. Conversely, if they feel like their voices are
not being listened to, or are actively being silenced, their
health and wellbeing will soon deteriorate. Whilst Mutable
Geminians are usually happy to go along with the plans of
others, it's integral that they make their imprint in some way if
they are to be true to themselves and feel content.

As much as Geminians advocate diversity in their lives, they
should similarly celebrate the complicated diversity within
themselves. They can be accused of being dishonest, but their
duality is an important part of their uniqueness that they
should learn to embrace. Capable of being the life and soul of
a party, Geminians can also be prone to feeling overwhelmed,
and may experience bouts of depression. Their social sides
should be exercised as much as their quieter, thoughtful selves
to help maintain emotional balance. Geminians should try to
surround themselves with friends and family that allow them
to show off their charming face and challenge their intellect.
Ultimately, they should strive to find a balance and avoid
feelings of depression by enjoying all sides of their changeable
personalities.

Geminians can be eager to move on quickly from things,
including their feelings. They like to remain light-hearted and
can be guilty of skimming the surface only. Delving deeply into
their emotions might initially feel suffocating to Geminians,
however the practice of looking at their deepest emotions

and desires can lead them away from living a purely shallow existence. By pausing and focusing more time and energy into themselves and their relationships, Geminians can often twice reap the rewards that they are used to receiving from their more impatient behaviour.

The part of the human body associated with Gemini is the nervous system. It ensures the body acts in the way that the brain tells it to, which is perhaps why communication is so closely connected to this sign. Geminians can push themselves mentally and physically to the point of exhaustion if they choose to ignore signals from their bodies telling them to slow down. However, they will usually only listen to pain before any lasting damage is done. Whilst it is not in their nature to slow down, even energetic Geminians will tire eventually. They may be able to pre-empt a burnout by taking the time to switch off from the constant chatter of their outside life and focus on their internal health. Regular screen breaks and going offline from technology could give their overactive minds a much-needed rest. A peaceful retreat somewhere with terrible phone reception and no internet signal may be just what the doctor ordered.

Gemini

....

DAILY FORECASTS
for 2020

OCTOBER
. . . .

Thursday 1st
Today's Full Moon in Aries is an extra powerful one, as it coincides with Mars retrograde. This will shine the spotlight on your social groups and communities. Conflicts may also be highlighted, but just for the purpose of resolving them. If you can agree to disagree, all will be fine.

Friday 2nd
The time has come to beautify your home and family life. This could range from a couple of simple touches to total refurbishment and redecoration, or simply doing an activity such as an outing which will improve family relations. Whatever you make this about, strive to achieve the perfect balance of form and function for the best results.

Saturday 3rd
You might find that some me-time is in order. You will be in the mood for solitude and the chance to sit quietly with your thoughts. As you relax, you may start to consider what you need in your home to feel happy, safe and nurtured. You may even feel inspired to make changes right away. Try sitting down with a notebook to help record your thoughts.

Sunday 4th
There could be a tendency to hide away today. As you try to align your heart and mind, you might be surprised by the effort it would take to leave your comfort zone. Are you willing to at least try? You may prefer to ponder it a little longer, but try not withdraw too much or get caught in a rut.

Monday 5th

With a recent transformation having taken place, Pluto is getting ready to set you free of any further investigations into your feelings and changes you might need. He will still continue to linger in this space, but you will feel that your evolution and development are now much more defined.

Tuesday 6th

The Gemini Moon puts the focus squarely on you. Or should that be you two, owing to your dualistic nature? You will enjoy posing questions about yourself, but it will be even more fun to discuss those questions with others. There are two sides to every coin, after all. Enjoy a time of self-discovery.

Wednesday 7th

Here it is, the liberating thought that offers you freedom. You will need to balance it with your day-to-day routine, but it will make for fascinating thinking. Your main task is to write it down and consider it more deeply. It might take quite an obvious shape, but it could also be quite subtle or hidden in plain sight. Be open and receptive.

Thursday 8th

'Receiving' is today's keyword. What are you allowing yourself to receive? Do you let someone else care for you or do you prefer to nurture yourself? This may also relate to how you look after your physical body, as well as your diet and exercise regime. Alternatively, this may be about mental or emotional care. How can you improve your routines?

Friday 9th

Today's energy might feel intense. You may want to act impulsively when presented with a question about power, but ask yourself if it is really worth it. Would you benefit from taking a big breath and counting to ten before responding? Avoid making any quick decisions, rash actions or jump to any sudden conclusions today.

Saturday 10th

A sudden event may change your perspective completely. You may be considering ways of improving your home and family life, and today could bring new insight. You may now decide to move home completely or want to rethink an entire decoration scheme. Talk it through before you act and don't make any impulsive commitments.

Sunday 11th

You want to bring balance and harmony to your closest relationship, and this may ironically be best achieved through conflict. The difference of opinion may be about childcare or housework, but airing these grievances will help you and your significant other to resolve them, and strengthen your bond as well as making a happier long-term agreement going forward.

Monday 12th

Do you need more encouragement to express yourself? Have you completed any craft of writing projects? You may have had so many new ideas that you were unable to finish a single one. However you respond to these questions doesn't really matter. Write, talk, make, create and express yourself today.

Tuesday 13th

Today is a big test. A test of your friends and social groups. It is a time to take action, and this may involve leaving people behind that no longer interest you or have the right influences in your life. You will be looking for new and exciting friends who catch your interest to fill the void.

Wednesday 14th

Another Mercury retrograde is ahead. This time, your planetary ruler is moving backwards through Scorpio. This gives you plenty of time to now re-evaluate your health, habits and day-to-day routines. You will reach interesting conclusions if you are prepared to dive deep.

Thursday 15th

Intensity ahead! You are trying to solve the tension between harmony, fairness and manipulation. It is one thing to give freely, but quite another thing entirely to give in order to receive. You need to be very honest with yourself. Are you giving to give or are you giving to receive?

Friday 16th

Today marks a New Moon in Libra. This New Moon is all about your joys and passions, and the way you express them creatively and with others. If there are children in your life, spend some quality time with them today. You may be deeply inspired by their enthusiasm and curiosity. Get playful or make some mess on paper or in the kitchen.

Saturday 17th

As the Moon enters your sixth house, you will return to
your day-to-day routines and familiar habits. With the Moon
crossing over retrograde Mercury, it is possible that you will
have the first real insight into what habits you want to change
and why. There may even be a habit you were completely
unaware of until now. Be prepared to see yourself in new light.

Sunday 18th

Today asks for you to become aware of the relationship
between your passions and your responsibilities. Is there a
way to change some habits so that they can allow for more joy
while you fulfil your responsibilities? It doesn't have to be one
or the other. Find a balance which is right for you and those
around you.

Monday 19th

Relationships are a theme today, and, on the one hand, there
are beautiful developments happening in your home and
family life. At the same time, however, something feels amiss
regarding your friends and social groups. It is not easy to cover
all bases, even for a Gemini like you. Take a step back and try
to see the bigger picture, perhaps from a different perspective.

Tuesday 20th

You may have a sudden insight today into a habit you wish to
break. It is possibly something you have been doing for the
sole purpose of appeasing others, rather than because it suits
you. It might just because it's the way you've always done
things. What would serve your own needs much better?

Wednesday 21st

You have been making such fantastic progress lately in trusting others, and the day will be drenched in loving connections as a result. This is likely to be with your family, or possibly someone you refer to as family, such as a dear friend or pet. Enjoy this time.

Thursday 22nd

As the Sun enters Scorpio, the emphasis is put on adjusting your health and nutrition, as well as your day-to-day routines. The next thirty days will help you to implement all the things you've been thinking about since Mercury moved into this sign. Get out your diary and put a plan in place if it's helpful.

Friday 23rd

The Moon is now in Aquarius, and you will likely feel some wanderlust. You know that a trip away will be great for your family, but will it be detrimental to all the changes you are about to make with your health, not to mention in any other areas? Will you be able to resist the urge to indulge if you go on holiday? Weigh up all the factors before you make any decisions.

Saturday 24th

You sometimes have a hard time making long-term commitments in your personal life. However, you're in a position where you actually can today, and will do so from the heart. As you make your promises, you will be relieved to find that you do not feel pushed or trapped in any way. This is progress.

Sunday 25th

Today Mercury, your planetary guide, will meet with the Sun. You will be able to merge all your preliminary thoughts with your current reality, and there will be a shift towards a more embodied experience. All of this will prove very useful for helping you to implement change.

Monday 26th

The week begins on a happy note, as your emotions align with your entire being. This day promises some excitement, which suits your mood. Not everyone around you will be feeling quite as upbeat, however, so why not be the person to light up the day? There are those who will benefit, even if it doesn't seem like it at the time.

Tuesday 27th

As the Moon crosses Neptune, you are likely to be restless and easily distracted. You will do your best to focus, but it might be wiser to admit defeat and work a shorter day. Once back at home, try to occupy yourself with a favourite hobby until the mood passes. You might bounce from one thing to another and feel dissatisfied, but remind yourself that this is acceptable today.

Wednesday 28th

You will feel driven to find a balance today. You may be tempted to dig your heels in on a matter, but that would certainly not support your need for harmony. Instead, take a step back from your emotions to explore what is behind them. This is the best way for you to achieve the balance you crave.

Thursday 29th

Your friends may hit a nerve today. You are unlikely to tell them about it, which may begin a difficult dialogue with yourself instead. Don't judge or blame yourself. You are having a human experience, and everybody has something they are sensitive about. Your task is just to be aware of it.

Friday 30th

Today may start awkwardly, as there could be some tension in the air. This is not necessarily bad, however, as you are likely to find a creative solution hidden within conflict. As the day progresses, the energy will ease. Allow yourself some much-needed me-time. The clouds shall pass.

Saturday 31st

This year, Halloween is tied to a very powerful Full Moon in Taurus. Whatever your plans are today, they are likely to turn out very differently. Trick or treat? You just don't know what you're going to get. Be prepared for things not to go strictly according to plan, but also let things open up in new, unexpected directions. You might be surprised at the results.

NOVEMBER

. . . .

Sunday 1st

November is here, and it brings with it a spirit of revelation. As the Moon is enjoying a smooth conversation with Jupiter, you should expect a happy surprise. You may receive a windfall, or it might be that you find a treasure you thought you had lost. It might not even be something physical, but prepared for something to come to you.

Monday 2nd

You start the day in a quiet mood, but with an inner stability and peace. The pace will soon start to pick up speed, and you will have many good talks and connections. If you can remain in a grounded mood, the day will indeed be rich.

Tuesday 3rd

You will finally be able to combine your joys and passions with the communities and groups you are engaging with. It is possible you may join a brand-new group that feels more in sync with your personality and values. Alternatively, you may start to express yourself more in an existing group, so that your experience deepens.

Wednesday 4th

Congratulations, you have made it through the final Mercury retrograde of the year. Today may bring a glimpse of where the future is leading you. Is it where you are hoping to go? Are you ready and prepared for it? Do you need to make any changes first?

Thursday 5th

You might be tempted to spend a lot of money today, particularly on something that would bring you comfort. It could be a cashmere blanket or silk sheets. However, it is quite possible that you will have changed your mind by tomorrow. Save your cash and sleep on it.

Friday 6th

Money issues may come up today, and it is possible that you will not want to invest as much in your social groups as they demand. Take a closer look at what they are asking. Is it really too much? What value does it have that money can't buy? Try to take a balanced view and see the other perspectives today.

Saturday 7th

Usually, you enjoy an amazing energy whenever the Moon shifts into Leo. You feel inspired and are willing to communicate and connect on your highest level. Today is no different, and you will love all the ideas that are flying around. Try to write down the best ones, at least. You don't have to act on the inspiration today, but it's there for the taking.

Sunday 8th

The Moon is still in Leo, but now faces tension from the Sun. This may manifest as a lesson about the importance of taking care of yourself. You can only cope with being busy if you give your body something it can work with. Why not cook a meal with friends to relax?

Monday 9th

Your focus will turn to home and family today, and you will probably be trying to make time for the children in your life. It might be that you need to take one of your own children along on errands, or you want to start a new tradition or hobby with a niece or nephew. Create some memories to be cherished.

Tuesday 10th

Mercury is about to enter Scorpio and has collected all sorts of ideas about balancing your day-to-day routines. The universe is urging you to think deeply about your health and habits, and wants to help set you up in a new way. This seems to be a recurring theme, lately, so take it seriously.

Wednesday 11th

This is a good day to have one-to-one conversations. You probably won't go out and will stay at home instead, which will allow you to go deep into devotion with that special someone. This can be a day of bonding, bliss and tenderness. Use it well.

Thursday 12th

There it is, the final meeting Jupiter and Pluto for a while. They won't meet again for over a decade. Together, they are trying to combine your highest and lowest needs and desires to set you up for further expansion and growth. You have made tremendous shifts so far, and this marks another starting point of a new attitude.

Friday 13th

You still need to catch up with your new attitude emotionally, and that is what you will be trying to do today. There is a sense of edginess, but this will pass by soon. You can actually soften the edges by doing something good for your body, or by taking care of your home. Take an introspective glance and listen carefully for what you need.

Saturday 14th

Mars retrograde is over. You have had to re-evaluate your own behaviour and that of others in your social groups. Mars will continue to highlight this area, even at the start of 2021. For now, you can focus on engaging with your friends, as there are only little adjustments to be made.

Sunday 15th

The New Moon in Scorpio offers you the opportunity to make the necessary shifts and adjustments regarding your health and fitness. This topic has come up quite a lot recently, and now is the perfect time to make some resolutions. Create a plan and stick to it. This could see a real turning point for you right now.

Monday 16th

You are so creative, but are you also willing to put in the work needed to shine as bright and big as you can? Sometimes, you need to stick with something in order to gain influence or even be recognised. With today's energy, you can make it happen – if it is something that really makes your heart sing.

Tuesday 17th

Mercury and Uranus have been arguing a lot lately and they are coming back together for another round. There is a chance it will be very inspiring, or will allow you to show your rebellious nature. You could surprise others as much as you could surprise yourself. If you get a spark today, just go with it.

Wednesday 18th

You could struggle with an issue in your social groups today. Your friends may ask you to commit to something, but you will feel a strong resistance from within. Do you really want to stick with that resistance or do you want to become involved more deeply? You'll need to think carefully about what you want and why.

Thursday 19th

The Sun is in a very positive flow to Saturn, helping you to pour self-discipline into any new healthy habits which you've been trying. It could be something as simple as a regular walk outside, but it hopefully involves changes to your diet. Even small adjustments can go a long way, today will help in making them last.

Friday 20th

Your emotions are in conflict with your mental energy, and you are still trying to weigh up the pros and cons of creating routine versus your sense of adventure. It does not need to be so difficult. Try to think of smaller routines that are easy to implement wherever you may be.

Saturday 21st

The Sun moves into Sagittarius, highlighting your relationships. You should expect some important developments now. Elsewhere, Venus, the goddess of love, moves into Scorpio, where she is able to bring beauty to the health habits you have been working on lately. This could all come together quite nicely, if you commit and give it time.

Sunday 22nd

It is understandable if you find today's energy too fast-paced. There are two planets at the very first degree, so you are probably just adjusting to the change. Luckily, it is Sunday so you can take it easy. Dive into daydreams, movies and fantasies. Let yourself and unwind today; it's not a crime.

Monday 23rd

The dreamy vibe continues on this Monday. You will probably be surrounded by many people, when all you want to do is just be with your loved ones or even by yourself. However, this would be a great day to go to a concert, play or the ballet. This would support all the energies, not to mention be a great start to the week.

Tuesday 24th

There is a sense of healing in the air today. As you start to implement your new habits, you will finally see how they can help you to draw boundaries with others. This is especially true for the social groups and friends you are interacting with. Others may drag your positive progress back down, or cause bad habits to resurface, even though they might not mean to.

Wednesday 25th

You will have lots of energy available to you today. It is as if you could go non-stop from meeting to meeting, and then still have the energy to take your loved one out to dinner in the evening. As long as you feel your energy is high, just enjoy it.

Thursday 26th

'Impatience' could be today's keyword. Things may not happen as quickly as you want them to, and you may be prone to overreacting. If you do, people around you will certainly notice. You should be careful to hold your tongue, as you won't be able to take back those words once they are out. Take a step back and know that things will happen when they're meant to.

Friday 27th

Sometimes, you become stubborn and resistant to change. It is an inner resistance that does not serve you. You will be able to beautify and harmonise yourself and your life if you can let that resistance go. Once you do, you'll see how much you will profit from the change.

Saturday 28th

Saturday starts with a nice, easy energy, and you can expect a wonderfully quiet weekend. This is a great time for wellness, comforting food and relaxation. If you can also be with a loved one, you'll probably like it even more. Use this time to recharge if you are on your own.

Sunday 29th

The easy and relaxing vibe continues, and you could include meditation in your schedule. There are many forms of meditation that would serve this purpose, such as t'ai chi or qigong. Even writing in a notebook or going out for a walk in nature might provide what you need. Whichever you choose, enjoy the chance to settle your ever-flowing mind.

Monday 30th

The month ends with a powerhouse of a Full Moon: a partial lunar eclipse in Gemini. It illuminates the work you have done so far with your self-realisation, and sets a milestone. Be grateful and appreciative for what you have already changed and received, but stay mindful that there is more to come.

DECEMBER

Tuesday 1st

As you enter this final month of 2020, Mercury, your planetary guide, enters your relationship area. This adds to the importance of relationships in your life, and you will be thinking about them a lot. This process will be prove to be vital, but remember to include your feelings and intuition in your contemplation.

Wednesday 2nd

You should try to take good care of yourself today, and find a way to include your body in your sensual experience. Sometimes your mind is running here, there and everywhere, and your body is left behind. Try to be in the moment as best as you can, by focusing on your physical senses.

Thursday 3rd

Physical activity could be a good outlet for today's tension, and will certainly help to avoid arguments. This could be through swimming, dancing, skiing or perhaps hiking. Treat your body well, and enjoy the energy running through your veins. It is a great day to feel alive.

Friday 4th

The day may start a little uneasily as you will have to deal with responsibilities early on. Once the working day ends, however, a happy and joyful vibe will emerge. Your mind and emotions will be fully in sync, and you will be ready to have some fun. This could be an after-work party or a get-together in your neighbourhood. Enjoy it – it is a reward for your hard work today.

Saturday 5th

The weekend starts with a surprise, perhaps with someone saying something that intimidates you. Don't stick with this feeling for too long though, and take action instead. This could be by talking to that person openly, allowing you the chance to speak your truth and heal the situation. There is nothing to gain from inaction, only regrets.

Sunday 6th

Christmas is on its way, so you will most likely be having fun buying gifts or hanging decorations today. If a family member comments that it is too early to feel festive, smile and carry on as you were. This is a wonderful time of the year to express yourself and your creativity; embrace it and enjoy yourself. 'Tis the season, after all!

Monday 7th

Once your Christmas decorations are up, you may want to turn your hand to baking. You might enjoy cooking on your own, but may later want to share the results with your family members. Why don't you try adding a new twist to old favourites? Or why not introducing a new family tradition by cooking something together?

Tuesday 8th

It is an amazing day to get prep work done, as you will be able to focus fully on tasks. The next few weeks will be very busy, so you will thank yourself later for getting ahead of time and doing the groundwork in advance for the coming days. If the phone rings, you may want to just screen your calls and concentrate on your to-do list instead. Try not to get distracted!

Wednesday 9th

There might be a little dissonance between your relationship and business obligations. You should take care of business, but it should not keep you away from your loved ones for too long. Maybe you can bring a little fun into the mix? This will be easy if you let your inner child out to play.

Thursday 10th

The focus returns to healthy habits and the transformation you have been working on recently. You might not be able to see how it will all play out exactly because there is a foggy energy, but you will know on a deeper level what it takes. Try to focus on the goal, even if it's just a shape in the mist. You can do this.

Friday 11th

This day marks a major release point. You will be able to actively let go of a habit or belief that has been restricting your relationship experience. With this, you can create space for new, healthier ways of relating that will be totally in alignment with your values and identity. It might take a little bit of extra effort or energy, but it will happen if you let it.

Saturday 12th

The energy of actively letting go is still very present today, so you may want to get clear about it and maybe do a symbolic act. For example, you could try writing down all the old beliefs and habits on a piece of paper, before shredding or burying it. Alternatively, you could have a physical clear-out and look through your old clothes and books.

Sunday 13th

The Moon joins the Sun and Mercury in Sagittarius, so you are now also emotionally in the space of your relationship realm. It would be a great day to spend with your beloved or somebody dear to you. It might be best to do something exciting together, as this experience will tighten your bond. Be bold and have fun!

Monday 14th

As the year draws to a close, the universe begins bringing in big energies again. Today's New Moon is asking you to take the essence and gifts of your past relationship experiences, and let go of everything else. Start to seed something new here instead, drop the negatives and carry forward with the positives and the lessons.

Tuesday 15th

Venus, the goddess of love, joins the planets already in Sagittarius, highlighting your relationships. You are now ready to take further action regarding your beliefs about friendship and love in general. It will become easier for you to understand how your perception is affecting your experiences. You may need to recognise that, in order for things to change, you may need to change a little too.

Wednesday 16th

The energy today is transformative, and you may find yourself wanting to break free of all boundaries and limitations. However, what if the structures you are operating in are not as limiting as you think? What if you could actually use them to your advantage? Consider this with an open mind, today.

Thursday 17th

You might think that Christmas is the next big event, but it is actually Saturn's departure from his home sign of Capricorn. He is also leaving behind your area of intimacy, trust and shared resources, having completed work on your new foundation of trust. You may find that your energies and focus shift a little over the course of today.

Friday 18th

It's another big day, as Mercury has one last meeting with the Sun before the year ends. This always offers a chance to reset and to align your mind with your entire being. This time, it could also offer the opportunity to align with your new attitude towards relationships. Try to find yourself a little time to relax, reflect and recharge.

Saturday 19th

One big event is following the next at the moment. Today is the final day of Jupiter in Capricorn. Jupiter spends about a year in each sign, and during 2020 he wanted to give you a new sense of abundance, while also increasing your trust and intimacy levels. Has he taught you a few lessons?

Sunday 20th

Today is very significant. Jupiter enters Aquarius and meets there with Saturn. When these two giants come together, it marks the start of a completely new cycle. Their work in Aquarius will lay a foundation that Pluto can work with once he arrives in 2024. Be on the lookout for new beginnings and the start opportunities.

Monday 21st

Happy Winter Solstice! Today marks the shortest day and longest night of the year. In ancient times, people used to stay up and watch the sunrise. This day also marks the ingress of Sun into Capricorn, which means your area of intimacy, trust, power and shared resources is highlighted furthermore.

Tuesday 22nd

Today could be busy, and you may want to work out what action you should take next. Try not to become stressed, even if you have a long list of tasks ahead of you. Try to move forwards as directly as possible, and tackle the tasks that are most important. If it helps, make a list in order of priorities, and perhaps share some of the tasks with others.

Wednesday 23rd

Unfortunately, today could be as stressful as yesterday. Any tasks you were able to complete may need to be looked at again or changed. You will understandably feel frustrated, but it is important to keep a cool head. Press pause, take a deep breath and create a plan before proceeding.

Thursday 24th

If possible, it would be good to take a break today. Thoughts and worries about money and gifts may be troubling you. Don't be so hard on yourself. Christmas is all about love, and as long as you remember that everything will be fine. Focus on the time spent together and what you do with that time today; everything else should be secondary.

Friday 25th

Merry Christmas! May the surprises you receive be jolly and bright. May love light up your heart, and may conversations be inspiring and loving. May all that you give be well received, and may the connections between all the people around you be strong. Enjoy the time spent together with loved ones, be they friends or family, and try not to get stressed out about what you think is required of you today.

Saturday 26th

Can you believe you are in the final week of the year? Today is wonderful to dive into Christmas stories that highlight love, and to just have a relaxing day. Think amazing food, probably with a hint of luxury, and the satisfied silence that will follow. Use today to reflect and enjoy the afterglow of yesterday and all that comes after in the days ahead.

Sunday 27th

Today you want to get out, see other people, play board games, share the latest news and events and just be in your element. Do all of that. However, as much as everyone may enjoy your entertainment skills, remember to listen to their stories too. It's a time of year to readily accept as well as to give, after all.

Monday 28th

Emotionally, you will align with your future purpose, self-worth and self-realisation today. The Sun is also in an amazing aspect to Uranus, so you could feel a liberating sense of freedom that may foreshadow the future. The energy is high and you will probably be busy all day.

Tuesday 29th

The last Full Moon in 2020 arrives, and it is in Cancer. This highlights all the progress you have made regarding nurturing yourself, how you handle money and what you consider to be of value. You have put a lot of effort into this area, and can now finally see the first results blossoming. Reflect on how far your have come in this area over this last year.

Wednesday 30th

Venus will ask you today how you can bring a higher level of love into your main relationship. How can you strengthen your bond, but also widen the horizons? The relationship you desire combines adventure, exploration and the deepest kind of love you can imagine. If you can dream it, you can make it happen. You just need to think a little about how.

Thursday 31st

It's the final day of 2020. As you get ready to celebrate, take time to reflect on the tests, transformations and gifts this year has brought you. What was the most challenging event? What was the biggest surprise? Who was most important to you? Let gratitude lead you into 2021.

Gemini

DAILY FORECASTS
for 2021

JANUARY

....

Friday 1st

Happy New Year, and welcome to 2021. The year begins
with the Moon in your communications sector. As a natural
inquisitor, you are putting feelers out and connecting with
those close to you. The festive celebrations are not over yet and
you have many people to catch up with. You can be the life and
soul of the party today.

Saturday 2nd

At social gatherings, you can be direct and assertive. This
will include online interactions. You are not slow to express
yourself but can be pushy and opinionated if you're not careful.
There can be much laughter as you can fool around and be a
clown. Enjoy the last of the festivities.

Sunday 3rd

Your family sector is highlighted today. The Moon connects to
Uranus, who likes surprises or innovation. Late gifts will please
you. Put everything in order today to start the working week
on a good footing. Healthy family interactions show how you
serve others in your clan.

Monday 4th

The Moon sits opposite Neptune today, meaning that you may
be pulled into unrealistic thinking regarding the workplace. It
could be that you are still not ready for the New Year's duties.
Don't let yourself be drawn into doing other people's tasks and
duties. You can be the underdog at work.

Tuesday 5th

Your ruler, Mercury, sits with Pluto today. There is talk of change in your responsibilities. Pluto wants you to end something which is no longer useful. Your fluid nature should adapt to this easily, although there will need to be some deep soul-searching in order to do so.

Wednesday 6th

Mars is spending his final day in your social sector for now. Tension will surface and trigger you into action or retracing a social interaction which could have gone better. Is there someone with whom you must patch up a recent quarrel? Do so now before Mars moves on.

Thursday 7th

In your dreams sector, Mars gives assertive energy. Use this energy to plant seeds of what you desire. You will find that your hopes and wishes take on a different agenda. Secret sexual encounters can happen while Mars is here as you need to feel connected but hidden.

Friday 8th

The Moon slips into your health and duties sector and it is here that you can be too hard on yourself. You may have already begun a New Year exercise regime and are likely to push yourself too far. Beat yourself up if you must, but this is not going to help.

Saturday 9th

Mercury enters your travel sector and your busy mind begins to think about vacations for this year. Travelling with groups or for good causes attracts you. Venus lightens up your intimacy sector if you would only let her. Relax a little, love is favoured today. This may make you uncomfortable.

Sunday 10th

Today you may feel like voicing an opinion and being rebellious. There will be someone above you who may reprimand you. This will be a theme in your travel sector this year, teaching you huge lessons about how far to go, what you can say, and to whom.

Monday 11th

Mercury has his second stand-off with a superior in your travel sector. Saturn first and now Jupiter warns you to watch how you interact with others. These are your teachers this year, so take heed. You may lead a rebellion or get involved with unusual people from other lands.

Tuesday 12th

Your first test is upon you and your ruler, Mercury, may be shouting his mouth off or gossiping. You do not like your secrets being revealed but this could be the case today. Alternatively, you may find a topic you have been researching reveals its mysteries to you now.

Wednesday 13th

A New Moon in your intimacy sector helps you to set intentions regarding endings, beginnings, and shared finances. This can be a day filled with tension which you need to release. You may have to bring closure to a part of your life today. An air sign like you does not need weighing down.

Thursday 14th

Uranus turns direct today in your dreams sector. This may feel like you are on unstable ground. The energy is very mixed and can mean that manipulation goes by unnoticed. Say what is in your heart, even if it upsets someone close to you.

Friday 15th

Emotionally, you are drawn to thinking about travel opportunities which show you a completely new way of life. Long haul voyages to war-torn countries or volunteering to help with nature conservation tugs at the heartstrings. Might this be something you can plan for this year or next?

Saturday 16th

The Moon now enters your work sector. As a fluid sign, you understand the need to be flexible here. Eager minds like yours are valued for their ability to research and see different points of view. You will tend to be over-empathic and over-keen to please those above you in the workplace for a time.

Sunday 17th

Meeting Neptune, the Moon asks that you emotionally detach from your career and get more grounded with it. You could have too many threads that you are following and need to hold onto just one for now. Try to get clarification and choose quality over quantity. Inner tension can blow up today.

Monday 18th

You are more outgoing and social now. Sharing your new ideas with social groups is a great activity for you. However, there is still some tension and you may come to blows with someone who does not share your ideas. Trying to keep your private life hidden is difficult.

Tuesday 19th

The Sun moves into your travel sector. This will highlight your plans for this year and throw light on the best area of discovery for you. Group adventures may seem like a good idea now but will have issues as the year progresses. Deep conversations with a lover may not go well.

Wednesday 20th

Two troublesome planets meet up today in your dreams sector. Mars the planet of war meets Uranus, who likes disruption. You prefer to keep this sector hidden but someone may have infiltrated it and caused trouble. This influence can make you over-eat or drink too much.

Thursday 21st

Emotionally, you just want to be left alone today. Your mind needs time to process all that is going on. Influential people will be putting boundaries in place this year. You will feel this personally and may react without thinking. Lie low until this energy passes; it will not last long.

Friday 22nd

You know that there are big changes to be made and begin to consider this. You do not see the value in this just yet, but you will. Your head and heart may have a battle today, this can cause you some angst as your inquisitive mind has no time for sentiment.

Saturday 23rd

Do you feel more settled, today? This is because the Moon has come around to your own sign and this concerns your sense of self. Self-discipline returns and your urge to see dreams manifested gets larger. You are soothed and allow yourself some downtime to relax.

Sunday 24th

The future calls and you try to get a vision of what that looks like. You desire fairness and more structure now. Facts and statistics are what you understand and can deal with easily. Saturn at the early degrees of your travel sector asks how far you are willing to go.

Monday 25th

Mars and Jupiter square off today, causing tension between your dreams and travel sectors. You are eager to make things happen but know that there are things you must put in place first. By evening, you feel more like staying in the protection of your own home eating ice-cream.

Tuesday 26th

There is an underlying feeling that something will rock you out of your comfort zone today. Mercury will soon go retrograde so you would be wise to back up all your devices and double-check travel plans. Your ruler may go easy on you, but it is best to be prepared.

Wednesday 27th

Staying under your safety blanket can help you self-soothe today. While you are there, you are emotionally challenged by that change you need to make. This energy also suggests that someone is manipulating you, stay safe until this passes. Say and do nothing or you may regret it.

Thursday 28th

Today there is a Full Moon in your communications sector. In this sector, you can be quite the show-off or be a courageous leader with inspirational speeches. It is time to be the latter, even if you upset a few important people. Loving change or endings can be made now.

Friday 29th

This is a very good day to show what you are made of. The Sun and Jupiter meet up and combine to send you the very best of energy in your travel sector. Your outspokenness may have paid off and a bit of good luck comes your way.

Saturday 30th

It would be a good idea to check in with your health now. Time spent with family can be stressful as you need order and not chaos which drains you. This is a nice day for conversations that are unusual or for dreaming up wacky ideas with family members.

Sunday 31st

Mercury retrograde begins. This is the first of the upsets in your travel sector. Double and triple check all travel plans in the next three weeks. You need to make sure that all things are in their rightful place and have no time for daydreams or illusions now

FEBRUARY

Monday 1st

Venus enters your travel sector and will add beauty and harmony. She may also bring in some much-needed finances whilst here. Balance can be restored between work and play now. Aggravation from your social groups may disturb your inner world or highlight what needs to be brought out into the open.

Tuesday 2nd

Today, you achieve harmony as the Moon makes nice connections to the beneficial planets. Your inner world may still be shaky, but you must use this trigger as a lesson. There is value in being open with this area of your life, too. You like to show and tell in all but your private life.

Wednesday 3rd

Conflict between men and women is possible as Venus and Mars are squaring off. Once more, this involves your secret life and your outgoing adventurous side. This afternoon, you take a deep dive into your mundane duties and martyr yourself. Do not self-destruct, you are allowed time off.

Thursday 4th

Today may feel like everyone is out to get you. You are restricted by elders or teachers and wish to retreat into your dreams sector. Motivation fails you and you feel like a ticking time bomb. You must pause and reflect now before taking action. Listen to your inner voice.

Friday 5th

Self-discipline returns but can be overwhelming. You have many jobs to see to, today. This evening, the Moon enters your sector of relationships and eases the tension. Spending time with precious relationships is important now. Passion and a need to explore with a special person sets the theme for the weekend.

Saturday 6th

An outgoing Moon helps you to connect with others in a meaningful way. Certain people will inspire you and may teach you a thing or two. Your interest is piqued in the area of travel and acting for the good of the collective. Boundaries are strong and loving.

Sunday 7th

There is karmic energy around today as the points of fate are touched by Sun and Moon. Emotionally, you are pulled back to an idyllic past where everything was an adventure. Your rational self tells you to march on and discover pastures new using the skills you have.

Monday 8th

Your ruler is in the heart of the Sun and is silent today. Your job is to listen for whispered messages regarding travel and higher education. This can be quite a thrill to you, as learning something new is what you're good at. The deeper mysteries of life concern you now.

Tuesday 9th

Today you may seem trapped or manipulated. Look closer and you will see that this is another of those triggers asking you to make changes. A Gemini can be indecisive for a long time before deciding on something. What is your inner voice telling you?

Wednesday 10th

The Moon enters your busy travel sector and meets up with three planets today. This may come across as conflicting energies of growing, loving and being restricted. Be flexible and go with the flow. Sharing knowledge with like-minded folk is what you do best but be careful not to be over-assertive.

Thursday 11th

Your retrograde ruler meets the Moon today and it's likely that you will be unable to get your point across within groups. A New Moon in your travel sector is a good starting point to make goals and intentions to learn all you can from the planets sitting here this year.

Friday 12th

Are you a pushover when it comes to your career? What message are you sending out? It is possible that you give way too much and go the extra mile in order to please. Surprise yourself and others by learning to stick up for yourself more.

Saturday 13th

You may wish to spend the weekend lost at sea where no-one can bother you. Feeling stuck or not sure of your direction and purpose is possible now. Be careful with lovers, as Venus and Mercury meet up and words may be misunderstood. A lover's tiff is very likely.

Sunday 14th

Mercury now backtracks and meets Jupiter. Any troubles caused by Mercury retrograde energy will be big today. Double-check everything. Just as the weekend is finishing, you feel sociable and need your tribe around you. Enjoy a Sunday evening with groups and exchange ideas and experiences. This will do you good.

Monday 15th

You may begin the week with all guns blazing. A sociable and outgoing mood is aided by the planets of contraction and expansion. You demonstrate an equal measure of listening and speaking which for you, is a win. When the Moon connects with Mercury retrograde, you are balanced.

Tuesday 16th

Fun loving Venus helps you get what you want today. There will be some resistance either from you or another, but embrace it as a precursor to the change you need to make. This is beginning to feel easier and more natural for an adaptable sign like yours.

Wednesday 17th

The Moon dips into your hidden dreams sector. Why is it that you do not allow yourself the luxuries of life unless it is behind closed doors? You feel like breaking some rules today and may go as far as reaching out to the taboo. You might just shock yourself in doing so.

Thursday 18th

The Sun now enters your career sector and will highlight where you are too dreamy and unrealistic. You can have romantic ideals of what your career should look like and this takes you away from the hard work you should do. However, you are more assertive today.

Friday 19th

Trouble with lovers or partners can keep you on your toes. The celestial lovers are at odds as Venus desires to connect with others whilst Mars makes you keep everything secret and inclusive. You want to shock but also play by the rules today. This is no easy day.

Saturday 20th

You feel more at ease now that the Moon is in your sign. Problems that seemed too big for you to handle now don't seem so bad. You are reviewing all that has happened since your ruler turned retrograde and processing this with your inquisitive mind. Well done.

Sunday 21st

Mercury now goes direct and, as your ruler, he will make sure that any mishaps which have occurred will be put right. This directly relates to your travel sector and your need for higher education and discovery. You can look ahead now and feel that you are aligned with your purpose.

Monday 22nd

Today you want to feel nurtured and surrounded by your own
family, home and belongings. You may even try to bring some
of that hidden desire for luxury into your home. Show off your
taste alongside your book collection. Cook an exotic meal
this evening.

Tuesday 23rd

An emotional connection between the Moon and Neptune
help to take you out of your rational, logical mind for a while.
Neptune can lead you into fantastical thinking but you will not
be swept away with it. Comfort foods can lull you back into
childhood and a warm, safe place.

Wednesday 24th

Today you may need to look at your finances, particularly those
that you share with another person. Taxes, investments and
other such important monies should be double-checked now.
Perhaps there is a payment deadline you have overlooked.
This afternoon, your communication skills see you acting as a
leader in an organisation.

Thursday 25th

Venus enters your career sector just as you are having a bad
day. There are too many demands on you today because you
have made a rod for your own back and been too much of a
people pleaser. Venus helps to soothe you and shows you how
to value yourself more.

Friday 26th

You are showcasing your communication skills and may be making many short journeys to see people today. This evening, the Moon sits opposite Venus and together they discuss how much you do for other people whilst disregarding yourself. Family first, but not if they take you for granted.

Saturday 27th

A Full Moon in your family sector will illuminate how you are treated within your tribe. This will also focus on your health and show you where you have neglected your duty of self-care. Mundane jobs and routines can be shared; you don't need to take full responsibility.

Sunday 28th

A lot of earthy energy asks you to slow down today. As an air sign, you are always blowing around and getting things done but today, you must root yourself. Let your feet touch the ground for once and connect to an energy which is unusual, but good for you.

MARCH

· · · · · · · · · · · · · · · · · ·

Monday 1st

Creativity and higher education can go hand in hand. You are asked to find a balance between expressing yourself and searching for truth in the wider world. Right now, you are on top form and can see a future in this. You are beginning to sense your new mission.

Tuesday 2nd

Mercury gets you to look at your skill set and asks why you are not using it to your full potential. Your ruler is aiming to educate you in travel, communicating and doing something for the greater good. Listen to the voice of the messenger as he brings you guidance.

Wednesday 3rd

A difficult Moon has you being hard on yourself again. You take on too many duties and obligations to others and do not see to yourself. Consider your health at this time, as it is likely that your blood pressure is getting too high and you need to calm down.

Thursday 4th

Today you must insist on some time off. You are at loggerheads with someone in authority and need to speak your mind. This may result in a lost friendship or, alternatively, will give you the chance to talk it out and transform a relationship with someone in your social groups.

Friday 5th

Your relationship sector is in focus now. There will be tactic talk with someone in authority. Hostility can arise but you have it under control. You are firm but fair with someone who needs to know some home truths. You have no time for flaky colleagues at work.

Saturday 6th

Personal relationships can be very active today. Your natural inclination to talk is enhanced by Jupiter today, all manner of things might be discussed between you and another. You may be talking with someone from your past and reminiscing together. This is a fun day with pleasant energy for you.

Sunday 7th

There may be some chaos or mess that needs sorting today, and you know best how to do it. You need to be innovative with a touch of compassion and responsibility. You could be taken into someone's confidence and needed to help stop their secrets from being unravelled.

Monday 8th

Today's energy is very simple but comes with a warning. Make sure that people in the workplace are pulling their weight. You might be emotionally pulled to drift off and join them, but this is not a good idea. Be responsible and stay away from those who are not being fair.

Tuesday 9th

Staying in control today requires more effort than usual. You have the energy to go with the flow and get involved in study groups, but your emotions meet triggers in your dreams sector. Is this because you do not allow yourself to have too much of a good thing?

Wednesday 10th

The Sun meets up with Neptune today and burns away some fog or illusions around your responsibilities and the workplace. You have a greater sense of your work ethic and gain more momentum. This will not go unnoticed. Try to stay away from 'ifs, buts and maybes'.

Thursday 11th

Your heart and mind have a chat today. Try to still your inner voice so your heart can have its say, otherwise you will go around in circles. This evening you are more romantic and willing to listen to that heart of yours. Congratulations, you have managed to quiet your unsettled mind.

Friday 12th

In your career sector, the Moon makes a useful connection to Uranus. You may find it easier to solve a problem that has been bugging you. A different way of doing something may soon become the norm. Don't forget to claim the credit for this; don't let anyone steal your glory.

Saturday 13th

A New Moon in your career sector is a great time to think about setting new goals and making the first steps to climbing that corporate ladder. The Moon also connects to Neptune and Pluto, who dissolve and transform things. Use this powerful energy to let go and move on.

Sunday 14th

Your energy has picked up and your friendship groups are calling. Have a day with like-minded people and connect with your tribe. Venus and Neptune connect in your career sector making it a time of higher love with those you connect with on a daily basis. Arrange a work social, perhaps?

Monday 15th

The working week begins with you feeling bouncy and energetic. You have many ideas you wish to share but will need to bide your time a little longer. Mercury enters your career sector in the early hours. Prepare for brainstorming and networking on a grand scale while he is here.

Tuesday 16th

You may witness control issues in your social groups today. It is best that you keep your head down and concentrate on work. This afternoon you can allow yourself to dream up the luxuries you would like in your life. These can include what you desire to gain from work.

Wednesday 17th

Today you may find that you splash out on a little treat for yourself. Indulgence gets the better of you and self-discipline goes out the window. Something beautiful for your home or a planned solo retreat attracts, and you go for it. You could also be hiding money now.

Thursday 18th

The Moon makes connections to planets concerning love, jealousy and dreams. Boundaries may be dissolved as you connect with someone special or merge with a spiritual organisation. Be careful, the Moon's connection with Jupiter can mean that this gets out of hand. This could be one big illusion.

Friday 19th

Your sense of self and your appearance is important to you today. How you come across to others, especially work colleagues, means a lot to you. You try to please everyone but find that you are going too far and losing yourself again. Emotions may get heated as Mars is involved.

Saturday 20th

The Spring Equinox is here, and your time is best spent by pausing and reflecting. A massive re-set is about to happen and, as the Moon is in your sign, you will feel this strongly. You may not be ready for this, so take time to be still today.

. . . .

Sunday 21st

The Sun is now in your social sector. Venus follows shortly after and together they light up your friendship circles and bring balance, harmony and passion. You may even find romance amongst these groups now. This is a great time to begin new projects with friends under this influence.

Monday 22nd

Your home is your haven today, you seek protection and nurturing. Good old comfort foods will make you happy, as will connecting with mothers and maternal figures. Intuition is strong now. If something feels wrong, then it probably is. Spend time with a good book or research possible travel adventures.

Tuesday 23rd

You are unable to stay in a nurturing environment for too long. You feel stifled and controlled, but you want to get out and connect. This evening is the best time for this, as the Moon moves into your communication sector where you can express yourself and be heard.

Wednesday 24th

Venus is in the heart of the Sun today. As they are both in your social sector, this may be another episode where you feel smothered. Mars and Mercury (or your drive and your mind) are also at odds and you must be mindful of your words as they could be hurtful.

Thursday 25th

Your mind is full of chatter today, and you may not know whether you're coming or going. If you are feeling pulled in two directions, do nothing. Stay in the centre and observe from afar. Jupiter is making this bigger than it need be. This will soon pass.

Friday 26th

Today is best spent making sure all small but necessary chores get done. You have more than enough energy today to do this. Be careful that you do not stretch yourself too far. Family may ask for your help and you will be happy to serve them unconditionally.

Saturday 27th

Heavy energy does not make the weekend go well. This could make you feel unusually tired and you just want to switch off. Perhaps you have overdone the tasks and visits. Do not let it get you down; the Moon will shift and you will be back to yourself soon.

Sunday 28th

A Full Moon lights up your creative sector and shows you where your self-expression has led you. This Moon is opposite Venus and you may find that you have trouble in your love life or with certain female characters at work. This can also expose any unfairness going on at work.

Monday 29th

Nice connections today bring back a bit of harmony, making you able to say what you mean and say it well. Both Saturn and Jupiter—your biggest teachers—are rooting for you and will help you to use just the right amount of pressure without breaching any boundaries.

Tuesday 30th

Check in with your health today, as something may be bubbling under the surface. Head colds are likely – you must use these as a cue to slow down and take some pressure off yourself. A good friend will show you some compassion today, let them look after you for a while.

Wednesday 31st

If you find that you are carrying to much stress which does not belong to you, then dump it. This could be what is weighing you down and making you ill. Friendship groups are the biggest help to you today. Start looking after yourself better; take back your power.

APRIL

....

Thursday 1st

How you relate to people will be on your mind today. Both
the Moon and Sun have nice connections to otherwise harsh
planetary energy. You feel controlled and balanced in your
relationships. There is an equal amount of give and take which
makes you satisfied, optimistic and outgoing.

Friday 2nd

You will radiate passionate energy today. Mercury is in the late
degrees of your career sector and helps you to ask for what
you want. You have brave ideas and can get them noticed now.
Assertiveness is easy with Mars in your sign, just don't overdo
it and get pushy.

Saturday 3rd

You may feel guilty about putting your forward thinking out
there. Your ruler, Mercury, has your back and is assuring you
that this feeling is not necessary. As the Moon shifts, so does
your mood and you feel ambitious again. This could also be
about getting to know someone deeper.

Sunday 4th

In your social circle, you may find that there are arguments or
disagreements. Locking heads with others can produce some
great ideas if you give another the chance to speak. In the late
hours, you feel like switching off and spending the remainder
of the weekend alone with your dreams.

Monday 5th

Mercury has now shifted into your social circle. Networking will be busy, and you may find new connections who welcome you into their group. This could be the start of a new selfless or charitable venture. You may also bring about an ending or gain closure on a deeply sensitive issue.

Tuesday 6th

You are triggered today and can get over-sensitive about sharing your dreams. The Moon meets Saturn in your travel sector, and you are asked to listen to others and learn from them. This will be useful at a later date. Romance is on the agenda if you play nicely.

Wednesday 7th

This is a lucky day, maybe you should buy a lottery ticket if it feels right. You have Venus and Mars helping you to get what you desire. Jupiter is also involved here and makes everything bigger. Be happy and Jupiter will fill you with joy. Take advantage of this great energy today.

Thursday 8th

In the workplace, what may be seen as your wacky ideas and thinking now reaps rewards. Your ability to look at different angles can sometimes be a problem. Not today; you can look backwards and forwards and pull out the best of both. Evaluate it all and reach for your goals.

Friday 9th

Today can bring some foggy thinking as the Moon meets Neptune in your career sector. What looked good yesterday no longer does so. You can get angry with yourself and not see the bigger picture. This energy will pass quickly; leave it alone for now and return another time.

Saturday 10th

The Moon moves into your social sector and signals spending time with friends. This can be highly beneficial for you, as it is blessed by the two luck bringers, Venus and Jupiter. Your ruler, Mercury, has you chatting through the night with someone who will become influential to you.

Sunday 11th

Mind chatter is at high volume today. This is familiar ground to you with your busy thoughts. There is a lot for you to process but you will enjoy this. Spending a Sunday doing research about a new interest will be the best thing you can do now.

Monday 12th

A New Moon in your social sector is a great time to filter out connections which no longer stimulate you. This Moon will fire you up to do more with the right people and discard the ones who waste your time. Do this kindly, let them go with love.

Tuesday 13th

Today, you need to get more in touch with your senses. A hidden part of you is waiting to explode and you do not wish to hurt anyone. A tasty meal, yoga, meditation or a walk in nature will do you good. You may overspend on a luxury item, now.

Wednesday 14th

This is a dreamy day where you may not be able to focus effectively. Your restless mind turns to the irrational and unrealistic. Venus is at the final degree of your social sector and asks that you make sure this area is in order before she moves on to beautify your dreams.

Thursday 15th

The Moon moves into your sign this morning. You become more self-centred and, with Venus moving into your dreams sector, you could be selfish in love. Venus here will add more sexy, sensual, private encounters. She can also help you dream up ways of making money for yourself.

Friday 16th

What is it between your social and intimate lives that is at odds? You must take a good look with your heart at what is causing this tension. Saturn will help you to work this out for the best. There may be subtle control issues going on now.

Saturday 17th

There is so much going on in the heavens today. You feel like a runner before the race as the tension peaks. This energy is action-packed, and you must use it to initiate something you feel passionate about. This could be hugely important for you; birth it now.

Sunday 18th

Mercury is in the heat of the Sun again and your job is to listen. Your ruler is getting new downloads of information and this is likely to do with yesterday's tension. Take comfort in your own home with favourite foods and nurture yourself today, just as an expectant mother would.

Monday 19th

There is a double whammy of planetary shifts today. Both Mercury and the Sun enter your dreams sector. This is great news. Your purpose could become clearer now as Mercury flies around in your hidden realm, looking for the gold deep in your psyche. Enjoy this time of enlightenment.

Tuesday 20th

You have a crisis of conscience today. There are some things you believe should stay personal and private, yet there is the urge to share and learn from this purpose that Mercury is bringing up. Believe that triggers are there for a reason; let that grit become your pearl.

Wednesday 21st

Today you are still feeling unsettled. You must pause and put your emotions into perspective and look at where they are coming from. You have the ability to express yourself with ease now, even though you may not think so. Be responsible and respectful to yourself and others.

Thursday 22nd

Mars is at the final degree of your own sign; you may find that you are overly assertive or in a rush to get things done. It is possible that you have something on your mind which will come out in the wrong way. Crazy energy will exaggerate everything today.

Friday 23rd

Family time becomes important now. Check in on those you have neglected recently. You may feel a little more selfish today and want your needs met above the needs of others. Venus and Uranus meet in your dreams sector, making a pleasant surprise or an unusual sensual encounter.

Saturday 24th

Duty and service are the issues for today. This will involve parenting roles and show where you are nurturing and where you are the responsible person in your household. Surreal conversations will make you pay attention this evening. Your energy is easily drained today; get enough rest and avoid conflict.

Sunday 25th

A harmonising Moon in your creative sector gets a useful nudge from Saturn. You may be balancing out what you can learn and what you can teach. Words of love can be sweet but be careful that this is not gentle manipulation from someone you prefer to keep secret.

Monday 26th

Today you dive straight into your mundane duties and relentlessly push yourself. This is the area where you are prone to self-destructive tendencies. Self-control fuels you to do your very best by everyone except yourself. Check in with your health, now; overdoing things can lead you to burn out very quickly.

Tuesday 27th

A Full Moon in your health and duties sector will highlight how far you go for others. This Moon makes some edgy connections to other planets, leaving you to feel misunderstood or used. You will want to have your say about this, and your evil twin may come out of the shadows.

Wednesday 28th

The planet of permanent change, Pluto, turns retrograde today. This will be for a few months in your intimacy sector. Coming off the back of the Full Moon, you may see a hint of what is about to be transformed or ended in the coming months.

Thursday 29th

Your opposite sign is home to the Moon now. Your relationships will be in focus, but so will the relationship you have with the shadow side of yourself. You may find that you are looking to the past for a clue on how to deal with a tricky situation. You should be looking at the future.

Friday 30th

Difficult energy makes today one you might wish to forget. Secrets may be exposed, and you feel violated. Something you once thought of as a beautiful dream may now become your worst nightmare. Calm down, you can handle this; use your powers of communicating effectively.

MAY

· · · · · · · · · · · · · · · ·

Saturday 1st

Running away will not solve any problems, but giving yourself time off and away from conflict will help. Revelations from your dreams sector may make you think more about what you do in the safety of your own home. You may just need to re-think or evaluate the worth here.

Sunday 2nd

There is a lot going on for you right now. This involves sex, death and rebirth. Transforming or ending something is likely. You must learn to let go, as the relationship to what you are attached to will never be the same again. This could also involve money.

Monday 3rd

The Moon moves into your travel sector and you have time to dream up a revolution. You are moved to do something for the good of a group or organisation. Join with others who are on your wavelength and come up with an ingenious plan to get away and be useful.

Tuesday 4th

Your ruler now returns home to your sign. Your already busy mind will be on overdrive for the next couple of weeks. Ideas of how to best express yourself and your calling will come flooding in. Curb your words, as your speech may come through unfiltered with Mercury here.

Wednesday 5th

Today you meet someone who will become influential to you. A spiritual leader or generous person will inspire you to act for the collective. Your mental activity drifts away from your work obligations and towards romantic dreams of missions and quests. Stay on task, there is room for this later.

Thursday 6th

Take notes of what enters your head now; you may want to try looking at all possible angles before acting. Jupiter is at the last degree of your travel sector and asks if you are sure about a project which involves groups, religion or the law. Ask for help if unsure.

Friday 7th

You will feel the weekend vibe before it arrives. The general mood lifts you up and plans are made. This could be a great weekend for romance and seduction. A secret rendezvous is likely which will fire you up with enthusiasm. Play safe and have fun.

Saturday 8th

Venus and Jupiter are not friendly today, and this causes problems in your social groups and private life. You may feel possessive and protective over your own space and resent intruders or pushy people. You can get around this with words and remain tactful. Protect your boundaries at all costs.

Sunday 9th

The lovely Venus glides into your sign to whisper sweet nothings in your ears. This is also a good day for romance but be careful that the Venus influence does not make you prey to manipulation. Keep your wits about you; take off the rose-tinted glasses and get a reality check.

Monday 10th

You may be in for a shock this evening. The emotional Moon meets with Uranus who likes to disrupt everything, watch out especially for unusual requests which make you uncomfortable. This could also be a nice surprise but either way, you may be rocked out of your comfort zone.

Tuesday 11th

Today there is a New Moon in your private sector. This is your chance to set goals and make intentions regarding your private life, dreams and spiritual connections. Your ruler meets the point of destiny, so you must listen out for any messages and signs showing the direction of your true north.

Wednesday 12th

You could be extra-emotional today. This can be a good thing when Moon meets Venus in your sign. Romance is favoured and emotions are more on the positive side. It is possible that you have fallen in love and have not yet come back to earth.

Thursday 13th

Listen to your heart today. The Moon visits the point of destiny and then Mercury. Your heart will tell you if something is right for you now. You get the nod from Saturn who asks you to go ahead and try. There is always a lesson when Saturn is involved.

Friday 14th

Lucky Jupiter enters your career sector now. He expands everything he touches, so make the most of him while he is there. Now is the time to consider career advancement and talk to the boss. With the Moon still in your sign, you have the gift of the gab and can negotiate anything now.

Saturday 15th

This is definitely the time to think about climbing the corporate ladder. The Moon connects nicely to Jupiter, from your sector of money and possessions. What will enhance your home life and make you feel nurtured? Make that your priority and ask Jupiter to bring it in.

Sunday 16th

Emotional attachments to your money or your home life are likely to make you assertive and aggressive today. Holding onto things tightly may make you feel secure for fear of being without. You ask yourself why you feel this way and try to get a different viewpoint on what is important to you.

Monday 17th

Your finances or taxes need to be looked at now. There is a good chance of a windfall or a saving made in some way. Venus meets the point of destiny and you look to the future and how you can bring in more of what you love.

Tuesday 18th

Expressing your true nature is tricky for a Gemini who has two distinct personas. When the Moon is in your creative sector, you are the child who likes to play and laugh. This may rile someone in authority who sees this as being silly and childish. Let your inner child play.

Wednesday 19th

Your heart and mind are in sync and you have a happy day.
Seeking out persons in authority or a spiritual leader will be
difficult as you do not have that frame of mind. There could
be conflict from someone from the family who disapproves of
your childlike playfulness.

Thursday 20th

This is your birthday month; the Sun now enters your sign.
Happy Birthday! Today you wish to serve and do your best for
your closest family members. Be careful that you are not being
taken for granted here. Venus softens the blow from Saturn,
who is teaching you about boundaries.

Friday 21st

Foggy thinking makes communication difficult now. The
Moon is making troublesome connections to your ruler,
Mercury, and to Neptune, who dissolves anything tangible.
Wait until this passes and try to get clarity another day. Get
on with household chores and tick off your to-do list, this
will help.

Saturday 22nd

The greatest planetary teacher, Saturn, turns retrograde today
in your travel sector. This is a call for you to consider any plans
you may have already made in this area. The next few months
may feel blocked or restricted. Use this time to slow down and
evaluate everything before setting off.

Sunday 23rd

Uneasy energy makes thinking unclear again. This could make you feel angry and out of control. Family issues or conflicts may surface. You must be creative and try to bring about harmony in a way that suits all. The role of judge and jury is your today. Be wise.

Monday 24th

Digging too deep or pushing yourself too hard is going to make you ill now. Slow down and understand that quality is more important than quantity and get the really important tasks done. You are likely to run out of steam if you try to do it all today.

Tuesday 25th

You are given extra energy today and learn to use your intuition more. Train yourself to be a detective now and get to the bottom of a deep problem or task which has been evading you. Watery energy makes your ideas flow into unknown territory and you bring back pearls.

Wednesday 26th

A Full Moon in your opposite sign shows how you are relating to people. Look at what you have achieved in this area in the last six months. What has come to fruition? The Moon also hits a point where you find yourself looking back at the past in relationships.

Thursday 27th

This can be a difficult day where you feel duped or tricked in relationships. Venus and Mercury sitting in your own sign make you feel vulnerable and misunderstood. Neptune throws a mist over events in your relationship sector. Wait until this lifts and you will feel less like a fool.

Friday 28th

Taking the small steps today will get you to the viewpoint you need. You require height along with depth and some width given by Jupiter. These will help you to see the bigger picture. Be ready to have an open mind. This might sound cryptic, but you will know what it means when you see it.

Saturday 29th

Venus snuggles up to Mercury just before he turns retrograde in your sign. In the beginning, this will feel unsettling, but you will realise that the next three weeks comes as a reset to outdated ways of thinking about your worth, your talents and your abilities. You have Venus' blessings for this.

Sunday 30th

Today brings less difficult energy and you find yourself thinking about a group adventure once more. Remember that you must evaluate the worth of this before flying off. Social events with friends can be pleasant and end the weekend on a good note, with a way forward illuminated.

Monday 31st

The Moon meets Saturn retrograde in your travel sector. This could be the first of the lessons you need to learn about groups and adventure. Check the financial side of any travel plans. Do you have the resources needed? Are you being realistic about this whole project?

JUNE

. . . .

Tuesday 1st

This is an important day for you. The Sun meets the point of destiny in your sign while the Moon meets Jupiter. You should get a huge signpost today, which will show you where you are meant to be heading in this life. Jupiter in your career sector suggests that this is work related.

Wednesday 2nd

If you feel pulled in two directions today, it is because your heart and mind are both processing new information. Anxious feelings surface but they are there to give you the push you need. Venus enters your finance sector and will help to bring in the necessary resources.

Thursday 3rd

Allow yourself to hold on to your dreams today. Emotional attachments to the old may have to go in order to make room for the new. You may have a crisis of conscience, but this feeling will soon pass. Worries about money and work will arise and you want to throw your dreams away. Don't make any decisions relating to this just yet.

Friday 4th

Remember that Mercury is retrograding in your sign and asking you to double-check absolutely everything. This planetary energy may feel like your vision is impossible, but it's actually making it stronger. Go out, ask friends, and get feedback from those in your social groups with more experience.

Saturday 5th

Today goes well but this evening you are filled with doubt. Trust issues come up within your friendship groups. Maybe someone is trying to throw their weight around and making you uncomfortable. Do not let them make criticisms on your personal visions and goals. It is up to you to follow your true calling.

Sunday 6th

You settle into your own environment and enjoy some alone time. There is no need to lick your wounds, as you have not been hurt. Jupiter and Venus help you to unwind and cast off any tension by enjoying good food, your own company and a little luxury.

Monday 7th

Still in your dreams sector, the Moon meets Uranus. Think of a volcano ready to erupt and this is you today. An unhelpful connection to Saturn tells you to play by the rules and keep a lid on those emotions. Mercury wants you to listen to your inner critic.

Tuesday 8th

A clash with someone in authority is likely today. The Moon enters your sign and you become self-centred. Energy, drive and control are on top form, but may aggravate a boss or an elder you would normally respect. Practise the pause before you respond to anyone today.

Wednesday 9th

The Moon now makes her monthly visit to the point of destiny. The Sun has lit the way and now the Moon asks you to invest emotionally in your new direction. Saturn in your travel sector is blessing you with discipline and responsibility. You can do this; make it happen.

Thursday 10th

Today's New Moon is an excellent time to consolidate your plans for the future. Any intentions set now will be sure to hold. This is in your own sign so you would be wise to use your powers of communication and research to vocalise your goals. Blow away any negative thinking now.

Friday 11th

Mercury is in the heat of the Sun and is in retrograde. Now is the time where you are asked to be passive and receptive to any new information you receive. Comfort yourself with visits to the family home or take care of your own needs with favourite foods and treats.

Saturday 12th

If a shopping spree is what you fancy, go ahead today. Venus in your home and finance sector meets the Moon. Together, they know that there is something you wish to purchase which will make you feel good. You may overspend on this, but it will bring you joy.

Sunday 13th

Guilty feelings may sneak in today and tarnish the good feelings from yesterday. You might be trying to justify your spending to yourself. This is where a Gemini, having two trains of thought, will get into trouble. Fix on one and discard the other; the damage is done now, so deal with it.

Monday 14th

Your communications sector is on fire today. There is opposition from a teacher or leader, and troublesome thoughts popping up from your deep within you. Getting your point across will be easy, but can cause tension due to Mercury in retrograde. You can come across as pushy and narcissistic today.

Tuesday 15th

Saturn, your teacher, is squaring off with Uranus, the disruptor planet, in your dreams sector. This will feel like someone is trying to block your plans for travel or group adventures. Remember that Saturn is retrograde too and is asking you to be sure of your boundaries and those of others.

Wednesday 16th

Today is perfect for dealing with all those mundane tasks that need doing. Detoxing your body and decluttering your home will make room for new growth now. You will feel resistance to doing this, or maybe you cannot find the time. Be sure to look after your health.

Thursday 17th

You may be torn between doing the chores and seeing to the important jobs at work. Procrastination does not suit you; you know what you need to do today. Prioritise if it helps. You may be prone to sulking if you do not get your own way now.

Friday 18th

A balanced mood returns to you as a reward for getting things done. Transforming and cleaning up your home brings satisfaction. You have the energy to continue with this today. The Moon in a fellow air sign helps you to think, rationalise and organise clearly. You become more optimistic.

Saturday 19th

This weekend, you prefer to keep a tight hold on your money. You are to be congratulated for being more self-disciplined today. Using logic to make decisions, instead of going with your emotions, is your more natural default and feels better to you. Well done for not succumbing to temptation.

Sunday 20th

Jupiter turns retrograde today and this heavyweight will slow things down for you. Having just entered your career sector, he will backtrack over the first degrees and return to your travel sector. This is your chance to open your eyes and mind and get a wider view of your visions.

Monday 21st

The Summer Solstice, the longest day, is here. The Sun has left your sign and enters your home and finance sector. This may feel like a good luck charm but with the planets Saturn and Jupiter in retrograde, you may need to re-consider your home environment and how you spend money.

Tuesday 22nd

Mercury goes direct today. You may find that, as a busy air sign, your ruler now has you running around and picking up the pieces that fell away in the last three weeks. The Moon in your relationship sector is happy to be there now and romance is favoured.

Wednesday 23rd

It is possible that you see a conflict between men and women or maternal and paternal figures today. For you, these will be in your two money houses. You must check on any investments or debts you have with another now. Relationships seem fated to fail but this is not true.

Thursday 24th

Today there is a Full Moon in your intimacy sector. You may have been growing a deeper relationship with someone and the flowering of that is showing up now. Alternatively, you may see old or pre-existing passions reignited. It will be hard to see this for what it is as you are unable to be objective.

Friday 25th

Another planet turns retrograde today. Neptune is in your career sector and whilst there he likes to dream and not get anything done. Your career advancement may have felt slow over the past few years. You have a short period to step up your game and clear away any mist or fog.

Saturday 26th

This morning you may feel oppressed and stuck. There is a need for you to take back control and make your own decisions. This afternoon, you feel like getting out and exploring. Fresh air and freedom, such as a walk in nature, will be good for you. Fill your lungs.

Sunday 27th

People are not letting you choose your own direction now. This is a time to stop and reconsider all options. Listen to those who know better than you. Venus now enters your communications sector and will help you to fight for your rights. She will temper your self-expression with compassion.

Monday 28th

A quiet start to the working week gently eases you into work mode. The Moon meets retrograde Jupiter and asks you the first test questions; how big do you wish to be in your chosen career? Are you in the wrong career? Find your purpose this year.

Tuesday 29th

At work, you find that you are weighing up all your options. You look at what worked out well for you in the past and if there is a possibility of you doing it again. What skills do you have that you are not using? Remember that inner-compass showing you your true north.

Wednesday 30th

The Moon sits with newly retrograde Neptune. Your heart is sick and tired of wasting time hanging around and you now want to do something about it. Neptune asks you to get a different perspective or ask for divine guidance. Put logic to one side and use intuition.

JULY
. . . .

Thursday 1st

Make an early start with your weekend plans. Venus favours
good connections and short trips to see people today. However,
Mars sitting in the same sign as Venus may have his own
agenda. You know what you desire for the coming days but
feel restricted by others.

Friday 2nd

Today should feel relatively easy-going. Your social sector is
alive with connections to the Moon. Conversations and plans
will be lively and energetic. Enthusiastic get-togethers will set
your mind racing and formulating new ideas you wish to share
and discuss. Your opinions are valued now as you'll find it
easier express them well.

Saturday 3rd

As the Moon shifts into your hidden sector, you allow yourself
some luxury. That could be as simple as some alone time,
much-needed sleep or your favourite foods and TV shows.
A connection to Pluto in your intimacy sector means that
there may be someone who wishes to share this time with you.

Sunday 4th

Your privacy may have been intruded upon and this can make
you angry. Love relationships are unstable and it is possible
that a row will erupt. At this time, you desire to get far away
from everyone and go on a solo adventure. Groups are not
reliable entertainment.

Monday 5th

Today you are more compassionate and reach out to others with your heart on your sleeve. Venus connects to the point of destiny and advises that you bring harmony to sibling relationships. You should be able to switch off and enjoy dream time or alone time without interference today.

Tuesday 6th

The Moon is back in your sign and hits your selfish spot. This monthly lunar visit gets you looking out to the future. You're likely to consider what it is you really need to feel safe and secure. Your ruler, Mercury, is squaring off with Neptune and asks that you stop dreaming and start doing. This may be a good time to start putting plans into action.

Wednesday 7th

Mars and Venus are working together now in your communications sector. Self-expression is one of your qualities and this will be useful in a love connection today. An older person you are dealing with regarding travel or higher education may try to oppose you or make you feel small. Practise diplomacy when standing your ground.

Thursday 8th

Today you simply must say what is on your mind. The Moon sits with Mercury and emotions merge with conversation. You cannot keep things to yourself. Getting your thoughts out will help you to get clarity on issues you have been holding onto for too long. Find a friend to vent to if you're afraid of what you might say.

Friday 9th

You may have the need to protect yourself, today. You could be defensive or run away and hide from a situation. This influence, with the Moon in your home and finance sector, might also mean that you are hoarding or refusing to deal with your financial circumstances. Talk to a maternal figure for some advice.

Saturday 10th

A New Moon in your home and finance sector is the reason you have been feeling anxious. Something has recently ended regarding this sector and you may have felt unsafe. This ending shows you the new beginning you must make. Set intentions under this Moon to make your home your castle.

Sunday 11th

Opposition from others in your wider circle and travel sector is likely to make you feel unsettled. Slow down and listen to your body. Why is this triggering you? If you are brave enough to confront this, it will be a good step in your self-development and boundary issues this year.

Monday 12th

Venus and Mars are getting closer and closer in your communications sector. The Moon will pass both just before they meet. This is a great sign for love. This could be a person who you enjoy lively debates with or visit regularly. Your ruler backs you up by also stepping into this sector.

Tuesday 13th

This is a lovely day for showing those you love how much they mean to you. Mars and Venus have met and exchanged love messages. You are duty-bound to serve the people closest to you. Jupiter asks that you look at the bigger picture and how you can be empathic.

Wednesday 14th

Surprises may emerge from your hidden sector. A dream can be shared with a special person who will be tactful and honourable. If there is something you wish to share which can be regarded as indulgent or selfish, then now is the time to do it. Have no fear.

Thursday 15th

Family obligations need attention today, as do your work responsibilities. It is easy for you to neglect both of these and drift into a comfortable dream world. You receive a nudge from Pluto to make a slight change to your routine. Balance duties and fun, now.

Friday 16th

Mercury tugs at the heartstrings today. Your ruler asks that you think before you speak. It may be that you are called on to be a mediator in a situation of unrest. Restoring harmony between two factors from your creative sector is important today. This could also involve a love connection.

Saturday 17th

A better atmosphere comes in as Mars and Venus both connect nicely to the Moon. Friendships and conflicts should now have quietened. This evening you will want to do something for yourself. You have surplus energy and need it gone; you can overdo it at the gym now.

Sunday 18th

The deepest parts of your psyche are trying to tell you something, today. Your hidden sector is receiving rumblings and is affecting your security. Boundaries may have been breached or secrets might have been uncovered. Either way, this will make you uncomfortable. It is essential to talk about this now with someone you trust totally.

Monday 19th

You have a chance to re-start a work project that did not go so well. Jupiter has retrograded back to the start of your career sector for a 'do-over'. You are able to see things differently now and this will be advantageous. This evening you are more outgoing and adventurous. Seize renewed opportunities and energy today.

Tuesday 20th

Mercury and Uranus make a great connection today for coming up with new ideas. You may have decided to renovate a part of your home. Impulsive actions and thoughts will be a great starting point for new home and finance projects. You might find an ingenious way to earn money. Don't be afraid to act on your impulses.

Wednesday 21st

Romance is favoured today as the Moon in your relationship sector connects to both Mars and Venus. The celestial lovers wish to conquer the world together and add optimism to your love-life. If you're single, then this influence favours connecting with others from your wider world and learning new things.

Thursday 22nd

Venus now moves into your family sector. Expect to feel her influence as a dutiful servant to those she loves. You should find that family members will help each other out more now. Also expect your self-expression, creativity and romances to heat up and get lively, as the Sun has moved to these areas.

Friday 23rd

Intimacy issues will be on your mind today. What you share with another is under review. This could also be that shared investments or bank accounts need evaluating. Have they come short of expectations? Do you need to cancel outdated subscriptions or monthly payments?

Saturday 24th

A Full Moon at the beginning of your travel sector will show how far any plans for group get-togethers have come. You will now see something, a possible flaw in your vision, being fully illuminated. There is still time to make adjustments here if you need to. This will only enhance your plan.

Sunday 25th

Uneasy energy makes you anxious or unsettled. Control issues or battles between sexes are likely at home and in the workplace. Finances may be involved and will need double-checking. Your gift of the gab can get you out of unpleasant situations but could make you over-assertive, if not aggressive.

Monday 26th

The Moon drifts into your work sector to begin the week. She meets up with Jupiter, the boss, and they discuss that project which needs re-doing. This will make you uncomfortable, as you realise that there is more to do than you first thought. Try to avoid being a scapegoat now.

Tuesday 27th

You are dreaming again. Your thoughts and inner vision are so clouded that you don't know where to begin today. Hang on in there, go with the flow for now until this influence passes this afternoon. This is one of those days when a different perspective is needed.

Wednesday 28th

Mercury enters your communications sector and will be putting you in the limelight now. If you need to make a presentation or showcase your talents, Mercury will help. A midweek catch-up with your social groups will boost your confidence and give you the push you need.

Thursday 29th

Mars enters your family sector like a sergeant major and needs to see order and not chaos. This may manifest as someone in your tribe being pushy and thinking too much of themselves. This, of course, could be you. An opposition to Jupiter means that egos can over-inflate now. Take a step back if you need to.

Friday 30th

As the weekend comes in, so does your need for privacy. You can be sharing a secret time behind closed doors with another. Alternatively, you could be keeping all the good stuff for yourself. Either way, good food, drink and luxury will be involved now. You may allow yourself to be seduced.

Saturday 31st

Processing thoughts and playing by the rules are the last things on your mind. There may be resistance from family or friends, but you do your own thing this weekend. You could become consumed by pleasure now, so be careful. Do not lose yourself in a fantasy world.

AUGUST

· · · · · · · · · · · · · · · ·

Sunday 1st

This can be a difficult day if you do not listen to your intuition now. Your ruler is in the heart of the Sun and needs you to be quiet. Use your eyes and ears to look for messages. You are likely to come up against strong opposition from leaders or teachers if you do not comply.

Monday 2nd

Ego may get the better of you today. The Moon is in your sign. Tension is high and, as a Gemini, you will likely find it hard to keep your mouth shut. Keep opinions to yourself until this energy passes. You do not want to come across as a know-it-all or a narcissist.

Tuesday 3rd

Today is calmer and you should feel the recent pressure released. You have got off lightly and can now process the last couple of days rationally. Lessons have been learned regarding your own self-expression and those of a group or organisation, the small voice versus the collective voice.

Wednesday 4th

It will be hard to concentrate on one train of thought today. The Moon makes connections from your sign to dreamy Neptune and expansive Jupiter. Following any one thought will take you somewhere you may not want to go. Watch out for arguments or revelations from your hidden sector.

Thursday 5th

Surrounding yourself with home comforts or even paying
a visit to a maternal figure will settle your mind. Your need
nourishment now. Familiar faces soothe you and make you
feel nurtured. Family favourite foods will be beneficial and
enjoyable. Let your home be your castle today.

Friday 6th

You drift back into fantasy land but feel a little guilty about
doing so. Loving connections with family members may be
just what you need emotionally. There could be some tension
between your own finances and possessions, and those you
share with another. Get real and deal with this tonight.

Saturday 7th

Today you are more outgoing and entertaining. You have inner tension
which you cannot share as it involves your private life. To compensate,
you can be over the top and act like the class clown now. Make people
laugh by all means, but do not ignore those triggers from within.

Sunday 8th

A New Moon in your communications sector shows that recent
tensions were part of bringing something to closure. This is
your opportunity to start again in this area. Reluctance will
not get you far, nor will sulking like a child. Say sorry, forgive
and forget, and move on anew.

Monday 9th

Today, the Moon meets Mercury and you are being asked to
listen to your heart. Get out of your head for a short while and
stop trying to rationalise emotions. The mundane jobs can
wait until your Gemini-head is back. You desire order now, and
not the instability of deep feelings.

Tuesday 10th

Your energy and drive to get things done return now as you are emotionally energised by Mars. You almost shock yourself back into reality and take a good look around before proceeding with the day. Your work duties are at odds with what you need to do for your family. Assess what you need to do before the damage happens.

Wednesday 11th

You have enormous compassion for family, today. You will be the people pleaser or the fixer who they all turn to. You may have a moment when you do not know what to do first; this will be resolved by evening when Mercury, the communicator, enters your family sector.

Thursday 12th

Transformations can happen today. This could be something as simple as re-decorating. Venus and Pluto are helping each other out in the areas of family and intimacy; relationships that have needed a shake-up could also be the subject of this transforming energy. Your input is important now.

Friday 13th

Be expressive, show yourself off but be rational. Finding the balance between showcasing a talent and being obnoxious is tricky, but you can do it. Today's energy is bright and happy, use it well and people will follow your lead. Your social groups will be impressed at your skills now.

Saturday 14th

Keep your health and well-being in mind today. Your mind and motivation are in sync, but you can over-do this and push yourself to the extreme. Remember that you have limits too. Saturn is reminding you of this and is keeping a watchful eye that you look after yourself today.

Sunday 15th

Another leader or person in authority is putting the stops on you now. There are changes you would like to make that you have only dreamed of so far. These may be taken out of your hands, making the change unpleasant. Perhaps you have not thought this out properly.

Monday 16th

Venus glides into your creative sector and you may well find your muse while she is here. Conflicting energy from other planets to the Moon makes you restless and eager for more adventure in your life. This can help you to put other plans into action. Go for it.

Tuesday 17th

It is time for relating to others in an honourable way. Your significant other or important one-to-one relationships will benefit from your wider vision now. Put unrealistic dreams to one side and concentrate on what is attainable. Reach out to the exotic and expand your horizons.

Wednesday 18th

Put any creative endeavours to one side and set your mind to work and responsibilities. This should also include trying to see the width and depth of issues which are more fragile than you can normally deal with. Take the small steps to learn about life's deeper mysteries.

Thursday 19th

Uranus goes retrograde today and you may feel this as a huge bump in your hidden sector. During this period, you are likely to feel vulnerable and fearful about having your private life intruded. Your ruler meets up with Mars and family interactions could get heated now. Keep a lid on your temper.

Friday 20th

Misunderstandings, wrong information or gossip are what you should be alert to today. Your own personal opinion may be at odds with those of a group or organisation. You may feel as if you are being controlled, manipulated or restricted. The weekend's activities will make this clear for you.

Saturday 21st

Travel comes back to your thoughts. You have not abandoned the idea of a group holiday or a long-haul adventure with friends. You may have to reveal something you would prefer to keep private today. You are emotionally guarded and defensive. This is the effect of Uranus now retrograde.

Sunday 22nd

A Full Moon in your travel sector helps to give you the bigger picture of your friendship groups. Plans may have come to fulfilment or need a tweak to be finalised. Mars and Uranus are in a great connection for getting something done. This will be a huge shove in the right direction.

Monday 23rd

The Moon in your career sector can make you feel drained today. Connections from Uranus and Mars, both planets who can disrupt things, make you edgy. If you feel pulled in two directions, stay in the middle and make notes. That is one thing you are good at.

Tuesday 24th

Words will probably fail you today. Your normal chatty, inquisitive mind feels like it is floating in mud. This is another one of those days where listening to your other faculties will be more useful. Your heart wants to tell you something while your brain is switched off.

Wednesday 25th

You are still experiencing brain fog today. This makes you very uncomfortable and agitated. Try getting out with friends today and brainstorming with others. Fresh perspectives can help you find your way through the fog or, at least, be pulled through by well-meaning friends. This can be challenging but worthwhile.

Thursday 26th

Disputes between friends or social groups are likely today. Control issues will surface and certain people will vie for supremacy. One person's opinion is not liked by another and a leader could get called in to mediate. However, that leader may have another opinion entirely. This will help evaluate the worth of your interactions.

Friday 27th

The weekend arrives and the Moon dips into your hidden sector. You may spend all weekend alone with your personal luxuries and favourite foods. Opposition from your wider social groups is likely but you remain aloof. If you are sharing this time with another, it can be very sensual.

Saturday 28th

Mars and Venus get connected via the Moon today. Uranus joins the party and can bring nice surprises or shocks. This disruptor planet sits with the Moon and can rock the foundations of your emotional life. This is not always a bad thing; a relationship may have gone up a level.

Sunday 29th

Until this evening, the Moon remains in your hidden sector and you are reluctant to let it leave. You are having a dreamy time and enjoying it. If vices or bad habits are involved here, please be careful. Neptune is also playing this game and can take you too far away from reality.

Monday 30th

You are safely back on earth and have come out of hiding, ready for the working week. Your private life stays private and your 'normal' mask comes out. Your ruler flies into your creative sector and helps you get to know someone better by asking all the right questions.

Tuesday 31st

Like a typical Gemini, your mind wanders between direct action and drifting into dreams. Once more you are difficult to pin down. Jupiter helps you out and draws your mind to travel and those group adventures that keep calling you. Remember he is in retrograde, so evaluate everything.

SEPTEMBER

· · · · · · · · · · · · · · · · ·

Wednesday 1st

Your awareness turns toward financial and emotional security. When you have enough of your needs met and there is money to spare, you feel safe. Sometimes this can be as simple as surrounding yourself with inexpensive things that bring joy. Your ideas may clash with others today, so that emotional security may be put to good use.

Thursday 2nd

Mars and Neptune are at odds today. This will manifest for you in your family and career sectors. How you are available for others comes under scrutiny. Areas of responsibility and general duties to your family of origin will pull you in two different directions. Meet your own needs first.

Friday 3rd

Emotions and drive are in sync today. You are able to balance demands from others and achieve satisfaction in doing so. There may be some opposition from your intimate relationships who try to control your day. This evening your communication skills are what saves the day for you.

Saturday 4th

Friction and underlying tension may be released now. As Saturn is still retreating through your travel sector there may be a conflict with a teacher. It may be that you have a differing point of view or a new idea that you have to get to grips with. Be patient and open to new and different ways of thinking.

Sunday 5th

At the other end of your travel sector, Jupiter asks that you reconsider people who you may think are like-minded but could turn out to be your adversaries. With both Saturn and Jupiter in this sector, you are being asked to expand your vision. Learn what you can and evaluate your social groups and friendships.

Monday 6th

The Moon sits in your family sector and you are almost holding your breath. Disharmony in the family makes you upset, so you must take the time to pause and reflect today. Hold that space between your own needs, those of a partner and also those of your family. This is no easy task.

Tuesday 7th

A New Moon occurs today in your family sector. You may notice that the recent tension has been alerting you to make necessary changes in this area. Something should have already ended and made space for the new. The Moon later sits with Mars who can help bring this change about.

Wednesday 8th

What are you passionate about? The energy now favours your creative pursuits and your love life. You can be more rational and logical when the Moon is in a fellow air sign but, as this sector is about expression, you are asked to feel it from your heart too.

Thursday 9th

The Moon meets Mercury today. Your mind and heart have a good talk and you know that you must learn how to blend the two right now. If there is something you have to say, do it with compassion. This may be difficult if people you are intimate with are involved.

Friday 10th

Your health and duties sector is ruled by seductive Scorpio. You always feel that you should go the extra mile here and exhaust yourself. This can be a sexy day as the Moon and Venus meet, just before Venus moves into this sector. Allow yourself to have some fun.

Saturday 11th

Be careful what you share today. The Moon is opposite Uranus in your hidden sector and makes you feel vulnerable. This can be a dreamy, floaty time, but you must keep one foot on earth and be mindful of who you share your deepest secrets with.

Sunday 12th

Today you can release some karmic baggage you have been holding onto. The Moon in your relationship sector also connects to a point which is about the past. Debris from relationships gone by may still be cluttering up your current ones. Make a conscious effort to let it go now.

Monday 13th

Exchanging words with a lover or partner is easy now, as you both have the same energy when it comes to talking and listening. The danger here is that you can lead each other into fantasy land and nothing tangible gets done. Stay on track in the workplace today and try to keep personal and professional separate.

Tuesday 14th

The Sun sits opposite Neptune and helps to bring you more clarity in your area of work and career. The fog or mist is burned away, and you may see things you have previously not realised were there. This afternoon you become more work orientated and responsible. Do some detective work now; you should be able to turn up answers and results you wouldn't usually be able to access.

Wednesday 15th

Mars enters your creative sector today. He will give you a boost in energy regarding your love life or artistic pursuits. You will be on a mission to express yourself and go after what you want. Mars will also give you the necessary skills to bring tactic talks and mediation into this area.

Thursday 16th

Today's planetary energy gives you the chance to climb a step or two up the corporate ladder. You should get through all of your tasks more easily and maintain a high level of self-discipline. Check in with any financial obligations you owe or share with another today.

Friday 17th

You may be at risk of burn-out, now. Short bursts of energy can do you more harm than long and sustained effort. Venus in your health sector asks that you take care of yourself today and get a health check-up. You are probably doing too much for others and not enough for yourself.

Saturday 18th

Spending time with groups of friends can be satisfying today. The Moon meets up with retrograde Jupiter and needs you to broaden your horizons or, on a smaller scale, open your eyes to those who may not be as they seem. Close friends will lift you and bring optimism.

Sunday 19th

The Moon has moved into your career sector. You will need to look at what your responsibilities are here. Perhaps there are skills you have previously learned which will come in handy now. Feeling stuck is possible but you are not so frazzled, and your personal health should be improving.

Monday 20th

A Full Moon in your career sector will show you what is going on for you in this area. Perhaps you have wasted time or opportunities and now regret it. This is a misty area for you, you have a lot that you wish to do but find difficulty processing this. Perhaps make some lists or use a notebook to increase your mindfulness and embark on some self-exploration.

Tuesday 21st

Social activities make your ears prick up today. Lively discussions and innovative ideas with groups catch your attention and your mind is activated quickly. Do not agree to join anything or begin something new unless you are sure of its value in your life right now. Think it over first.

Wednesday 22nd

The Autumn Equinox is here and this is a time where you must pause and reflect. Before the darker nights arrive, you must ensure that all that has gone by in the last six months is what you really want to keep hold of. Do not take extra baggage with you. Having a physical sort-out might aid you in have an emotional and mental tidy-up.

Thursday 23rd

The Sun will now warm up your creative sector and can also keep a love connection cosy. Be careful in your social groups, as there may be too many individuals vying for an alpha position. You may also be seduced out of your comfort zone and hidden sector.

Friday 24th

Someone may breach a boundary today. When the Moon sits in your hidden sector, there is always the danger of this. Alternatively, this influence can mean that you have an electrically charged experience which you prefer to keep secret. Make sure that all involved are comfortable if this is the case.

Saturday 25th

You can lose yourself in your own deeper psyche today. Neptune connects to the Moon, making you prone to switching off. This influence can mean that unhealthy habits are involved. Play safe and get lost in fantasy TV or books instead. Mars and Saturn combined should help you to keep your self-control, if you let them.

Sunday 26th

Mischievous Mercury goes retrograde again today. This could bring a few misunderstandings in your love life or in your self-expression. Be mindful of your words in the next couple of weeks. The Moon in your own sign can make you selfish or more outgoing than usual today.

Monday 27th

Today you will get some doubts from Neptune. Try to stay on task as your mind may drift off easily. A strong Moon in your sign is more likely to turn your emotional needs inwards and you will do what you like regardless. Do not neglect your higher duties now.

Tuesday 28th

There is a strong chance that today will see the first of
your communication mishaps due to Mercury retrograde.
Remember to pause before you react. Knee-jerk reactions will
make you appear foolish. By evening, you will want to snuggle
down and hide under the duvet with a tub of ice-cream.

Wednesday 29th

Your emotional needs come first today. There may be some
conflict coming from your love life. The good news is that this
may be overshadowed by seductive dreams and end in a secret
rendezvous. Mars energy is not always a bad thing, as it also
controls your sex drive.

Thursday 30th

The energy today is very watery and emotional. It will be easy
for an air sign to be misunderstood now. Air and water are two
elements which go where they want and cannot be contained.
It is possible that you will feel manipulated and you will be
unwilling to compromise.

OCTOBER

Friday 1st

Is it possible that you are scared of your own limits? You must confront your comfort zone and how far beyond it you are prepared to push. Are short trips and simple communication what you really want? Higher education into the deeper mysteries of life seems to be calling to you.

Saturday 2nd

You may see another mishap in communications today. It is possible that you show off or say something that you shouldn't. Jupiter frowns on you from your travel sector and makes you accountable. You are asked to consider your own ideals against those of another. You may not win.

Sunday 3rd

This morning you are more subdued and take comfort with your nearest and dearest. You have no space for chaotic thinking today and simply see to the mundane chores and outstanding jobs. Restless feelings can cause inner tension, but these will soon pass. Stick with it.

Monday 4th

Neptune's mist is shown up by the light of the Moon today. You are attracted to the unknown, because it seems to be a safer place than the real world you live in. Turn this around and try to see it as a trapping that is distracting you from your responsibilities.

Tuesday 5th

Pleasure is to be gained from a tidy home and a healthy body.
De-cluttering some mess will be the best thing you can do today.
As the Moon shifts into your creative sector, you find that you have
love in your heart for a tidy working space. Be proud of yourself.

Wednesday 6th

Yesterday's clutter was cleared just in time for the New Moon
in your creative sector. This is a busy day in the heavens,
and you are asked to set an intention to put energy into
transforming old things into something new and useful.
Pluto, the transformer, goes direct today.

Thursday 7th

Venus moves into your relationship sector today. Here, she will
bring beauty and harmony to strained relationships and initiate
new, exciting ones. This blessing will enhance love connections
that are built on a mutual need to explore the wider world. You
can be optimistic about love for good reason now.

Friday 8th

The Sun meets Mars in your creative sector. The next three
days will be highly passionate and driven. Your sex life will
benefit from this energy too. There will be a great balance
between your ego and divine self. The drive to express and
receive back will be harmonised.

Saturday 9th

There is a lot going on today. Sensual and emotional times
with a partner are likely. The urge to say what is in your heart
surfaces, but Mercury is in the heart of the Sun and demands
that you listen to voices other than your own. Past loves may
be remembered.

Sunday 10th

Saturn, your greatest teacher planet, now turns direct. A nod from the Moon in your relationship sector thanks him for the lessons about personal and collective boundaries. You are feeling much more grounded and steadier than usual. Breathe deeply and keep moving forwards.

Monday 11th

Today is filled with optimism and good humour. Relationships go well and you may even be in favour with those above you. This is a productive start to the week; prepare to step up your game. This evening you are genuinely interested in building something new for yourself. This could be a new career.

Tuesday 12th

You have come to realise that not all of your dreams need to be hidden. Do you fear failure or exposure? There is no need. You are admired for the way you think and process information and today, this needs to come out into the open. Surprise yourself.

Wednesday 13th

You're probably wondering where this responsible side of you has suddenly come from. You should know that you are not the airhead you think you are. Major planetary shifts have transformed your thinking and you now take yourself more seriously. Go ahead and show the world what you are made of.

Thursday 14th

Travel and group adventures are likely coming back into your awareness. The Moon meets up with Saturn and your thirst for the wider world now has more substance. You may decide to involve a partner in this; think about how this could bond you deeper to each other.

Friday 15th

How can one person make a difference? This is what you are wondering now. Something along the idea of a long-haul trip as a working volunteer or on a preservation scheme returns to you. Jupiter is making sure that you know what you are doing. Do all the research again.

Saturday 16th

The Moon will be in your work sector all weekend and offers you the chance to take time to pause and reflect on your responsibilities. You are aware of how this area of life brings dissatisfaction and that change is needed. Use your skills to push forward and progress.

Sunday 17th

Jupiter now turns direct in your travel sector. You will experience this as a return of optimism and the need to reach out further into the world. You are willing to make huge changes now. Emotional pulls towards a dream career will keep your eye on the goal, however intangible it seems.

Monday 18th

Mercury turns direct now; this is always good news for a Gemini. Communications will be lively, if a little self-serving. Put yourself out there; it is time to network and make your dream a reality. There is a big green light giving you the go ahead. Why wait?

Tuesday 19th

Your heart and mind have a talk and merge their ideals for your highest purpose. Understand that if your heart is yearning for something, then your eager mind will work out how to make it happen. You feel a boost in enthusiasm and mental energy. Keep it simmering and do not burn out.

Wednesday 20th

A Full Moon in your fiery social sector acts as a huge light bulb or spotlight. You may even have a 'Eureka!' moment and find the best solution to your plans. Be aware that you may be emotionally charged and a little bit resistant, but this will soon pass.

Thursday 21st

From your hidden sector, the Moon connects to Saturn and this energy acts as a spot check. Make sure there is nothing you have overlooked. The monthly lunar visit to Uranus means that you can be unstable today. You may be like a dog trying to catch its tail.

Friday 22nd

The Moon's connection to Neptune today may mean that you drift back into a fantasy world for a while. It is the weekend and there is a chance that you can over-do it when it comes to unhealthy or indulgent things like alcohol. Keep it safe and binge-watch your favourite TV show instead.

Saturday 23rd

The Sun moves into your health and duties sector as the Moon moves into your own sign and your sector of self. Use this energy to get in touch with your body and your overall health. Looking after yourself is of utmost importance now. Starting an exercise regime has a good chance of success.

Sunday 24th

The Moon opposes Venus who is sitting in your relationship sector. You will be torn between spending time by yourself and with another. This may cause some friction in your love life, so invite the 'other' to make suggestions on how to best take care of your own needs today.

Monday 25th

You have the necessary energy and motivation to get the working week off to a good start. Putting fragile and delicate dreams to one side may not be easy but do so and you will become more productive. Be proud of yourself; your wandering mind has been tamed and focused for today.

Tuesday 26th

Get into the routine of rewarding yourself after a good day's work. Enjoy coming home to your own home and a favourite meal. However, there may be some uncomfortable feelings being pushed up from the depths of your psyche today. Take note of the triggers and listen to what these feelings say.

Wednesday 27th

It is possible that issues surrounding mothers and fathers, or your possessions and those you share with another, will arise. It is worth double-checking on your finances as there may be money owing that you have overlooked. Career dreams and your love life are likely to be at odds today.

Thursday 28th

You will be tempted to show off today. Your knowledge base is highly commended, but it is not required. This will make you come across as a know-it-all and is likely to cause tension with people in authority or in your wider social groups. Venus and Jupiter can help to smooth things over with a lover.

Friday 29th

Your gift of communication and thought-processing works well now. Say what you want with less vigour than yesterday and you will achieve more. You may surprise yourself, as this will hit a spot in your hidden sector that makes you sit up and take note. Learn from this.

Saturday 30th

Family ask you to be flexible and need your attention today.
This can be problematic as you have plans for yourself and do
not wish to amend them. You must use your head and decide
which would be the best course of action to take. Which will
cause fewer problems?

Sunday 31st

Spending time with close family will make for a pleasant
Sunday. Everyone around pulls together to make sure that
chores get done, and no-one is overloaded. This could be a
family get-together with surprises or unexpected good news.
Be dutiful, join in and have fun with your nearest and dearest.

NOVEMBER
· · · · · · · · · · · · · · · · ·

Monday 1st

As the week begins, you have another boost of motivation. The Moon sits opposite Neptune and you can see from afar how your daydreams and unrealistic goals have dragged you away from your responsibilities. Get creative with your travel plans and speak to others who have more experience.

Tuesday 2nd

Your ruler is getting you to question the nature of the changes you need to make. Mercury is helping you see a balanced way forward. Self-expression is easier now than is usually is, and you are likely to come up with some bold ideas. People will applaud you for this new approach.

Wednesday 3rd

You are in a space of time where you can merge both head and heart and come up with the ideal way for you to make progress. There will be an emotional wrench, which could involve needing to end something big before laying the fresh ground for new things to develop.

Thursday 4th

There is a New Moon in your health and duties sector today. This Moon also connects to Mars, Uranus and Saturn. Whatever intentions you decide to make now will be fuelled by fairness, responsibility and the need to think outside the box. Someone important in your relationship sector needs your attention now.

Friday 5th

The Sun sits facing Uranus, and this can result in you feeling awkward and uneasy. Something you prefer to keep secret is under the spotlight now and you cannot escape. Alternatively, this could mean that you have been successful in dealing with something from your deepest parts and have healed an old wound.

Saturday 6th

Mercury is now diving deep into your health and duties sector. Prepare for some investigation or detective work into recent health worries. Venus will also be probing deep into your intimacy sector. Together they will help you learn to put yourself first and work on making your boundaries healthier.

Sunday 7th

Spending time with a lover will help to put more things into perspective for you today. This may not be easy, but you must remember to put yourself first. If the 'other' cannot respect your personal boundaries, then they are not on the same page as you. If this is the case, consider what you want and need from this relationship.

Monday 8th

The Moon and Venus have a meet-up in your intimacy sector. They discuss how you must take the small steps to climb the highest mountain. If there is someone you wish to know better, then you must take it very slowly and avoid burn-out. You will enjoy the slower pace now.

Tuesday 9th

The Moon meets Pluto and it is likely that you see a transformation today. The connection to Neptune suggests that you will see things from a different perspective. Neptune's fog lifts and you get more clarity. You may say goodbye to something which no longer serves you.

Wednesday 10th

There is a lot of difficult energy today. You may feel restricted or blocked at every turn. Leaders or teachers will not be listening to what you have to say. This could get aggressive, as Mars is part of this turbulent energy. Listen to your elders and do not react without thinking.

Thursday 11th

Today you can feel more outgoing and wish to connect to the wider world. It is possible that you join up with a group fighting for a good cause, such as a conservation project. This can fire you up to do something personally to help. You may even be outraged at an injustice right now.

Friday 12th

Your wish to help others brings you back to thinking about your career progression. This is another time to pause and reflect. Look at the experience you already have. How can this be used now? What new skills would be useful for you to learn?

Saturday 13th

Today you really want to make a difference. You have a sense of an adventure akin to the search for the Holy Grail. You know it may never materialise, but you are thinking about dedicating yourself to the cause. Mercury is teasing this out of you and making you aware of it.

. . . .

Sunday 14th

This new mission of yours could even be religious or spiritual in nature. This afternoon, the Moon enters your social sector and you may feel it would be a good idea to connect with groups to network and share ideas. You are driven and active now, your energy is high.

Monday 15th

You may have pushed a certain avenue too far. You are getting the nod from Venus that, although your enthusiasm is a good thing, it may have taken you down a route which is ultimately not good for you. Stop, breathe and evaluate the road so far.

Tuesday 16th

The Moon and Sun both connect to Pluto today and this can mean that control or power struggles have surfaced. Emotionally, you feel that this comes from your social sector, but it is more likely that something deep within you is struggling to be made conscious and you are denying it space.

Wednesday 17th

Your hidden sector is now visited by the Moon and you may feel that there is someone watching your every move. This is enhanced by Mars opposing Uranus, who both like to cause trouble. Be careful that you do not get aggressive today; there is still subconscious material surfacing.

Thursday 18th

As the Moon meets unpredictable Uranus, your mood turns inwards. You cannot deal with what you'll likely perceive is an intrusion into your private life and will be tempted to self-medicate on things like food or alcohol. Try to sit with your feelings and meditate instead. Your body is asking you to listen.

Friday 19th

A Full Moon in your hidden sector appears to expose your most secret parts. Be assured, this energy is simply asking you to get in touch with your inner self. Get out of your head and into your body now; physical experiences are asking for your attention.

Saturday 20th

Today you may feel more stable. Elders in your wider community, in education or from across the world have something to teach you now. You must learn to be quiet and receive wisdom. This will be difficult for a chatterbox like you who asks a lot of questions.

Sunday 21st

Your habit of switching off and dreaming comes back to you today, but you must resist it. Jupiter and Saturn are both in your travel sector and need your full attention. Educating yourself on a possible trip or long-stay vacation is necessary now. This will enhance your chances of achieving a new mission or goal.

Monday 22nd

Tasty treats or exotic dishes tempt you into a preparation of sorts for an overseas adventure. This is also a great day for romance, as the Sun enters your relationship sector and Venus and Mars are close to making a helpful connection. Make the most of this great energy and relax.

Tuesday 23rd

How can you restyle your home to bring you more comfort?
Think of it as getting ready to entertain someone special. Your
home is your safe place and it too requires attention right
now. Surprise yourself with a small makeover or a few new
furnishings without breaking the bank.

Wednesday 24th

You may witness an opposition between the sexes today. This
can be a transforming experience if not taken too personally.
This afternoon, your powers of speech and connecting
with others sees you catching up with those you may have
neglected. Mercury enters your relationship sector; prepare to
talk into the early hours with someone special.

Thursday 25th

Today you may need to watch what you say and how you are
saying it. This is with regards to people in charge or leaders in
a group. They do not want to hear your opinion. Do not take it
personally; this is likely more to do with them than you.

Friday 26th

Again, you experience tension with an elder, leader or figure of
authority. When the Moon is in your communication sector,
your natural inclination to share information can be tainted
with narcissism. Showing off will not get you anywhere. Time
to exercise the other side of communication and use your ears.

Saturday 27th

Family time comes around for the weekend. Here is where you feel safe to say what is on your mind. However, you prefer to see order rather than chaos in your family connections, so you are able to tone it down. Make sure that you do not let others walk over you now.

Sunday 28th

Neptune and Uranus both connect to the Moon today. Your family time may be spent sharing dreams and visions. When you have a get together like this, you can talk around problems with confidence and compassion. You may be the one who finds a unique solution.

Monday 29th

You're probably feeling that it is time to get creative or passionate about a project or a love affair. However, your ruler, Mercury, is in the heat of the Sun and is blocked. You may feel this as brain fog and wonder why you are unable to think straight. Get physical instead.

Tuesday 30th

Today you are juggling with a lot of areas. You have scholarly opportunities to take and discussions to enjoy. At the same time, you are trying to deal with fantastical thinking about life's mysteries. Try looking for a spiritual group who can help you answer these questions for yourself.

DECEMBER
....

Wednesday 1st

Great news; Neptune turns direct today. All that ruminating you have been doing over a career change will now have more clarity. You must continue to listen to your inner voice as your guide. Use more instinct and intuition now rather than logic. This is your future calling.

Thursday 2nd

You do not have to be a martyr. Being of service to others is a virtue, but not when it becomes more important than looking after your own needs. Conflicted feelings will cause underlying tension, which may erupt if you are not practising self-care.

Friday 3rd

Today can be pretty tense for you. Do something physical to let off some steam, perhaps with a good workout at the gym. Alternatively, brainstorm some ideas and theories with someone close. This can get deep and heavy, but you will enjoy it. Love is favoured for the weekend as the Moon shifts into your relationship sector.

Saturday 4th

This is an excellent day for romance and renewing commitment to someone special. A New Moon in your relationship sector introduces new beginnings in this area. Your ruler, Mercury, also gets in on the act and grants you the gift of meaningful conversation. No small talk, today.

Sunday 5th

Jupiter lends your relationships his optimism and wish for adventure today. Discussing travel opportunities with a loved one, looking at maps or watching documentaries will fill up your Sunday. You will begin taking the necessary steps to make a dream getaway into a reality. Enjoy this time with a kindred soul who thinks like you.

Monday 6th

Changing the way you have previously looked at something will reap rewards today. Intimacy will have a different meaning for you now. The energy is ripe for mutual bonds to deepen and transform a relationship. The Moon's first contact with newly direct Neptune brings attainable dreams at work.

Tuesday 7th

The Moon meets Pluto in your intimacy sector. This influence can sometimes bring control issues, but not today. You have taken the steps to make substantial changes in a difficult area of life. This is highly productive and brings you satisfaction. This afternoon, you are ready to share time with friends.

Wednesday 8th

You may feel strained or overwhelmed today. Don't worry, this will soon pass. You are reacting emotionally to the recent developments you have made. It is uncomfortable for you to be ruled by passion and not your mind. In this case, your mind does not matter.

Thursday 9th

If you are feeling stuck or hindered by people above you, lie low and just listen to what they have to say. Good advice can come from unlikely sources. You may feel victimised but, in fact, you are being guided towards the best possible path for you. Employ your passive listening skills.

Friday 10th

At work, you can be dreamy again and not fix on the task in hand. This changeable way of dealing with things is natural to you, which is why you often fall into it as a default action. Go with the flow, but do not overlook the important things.

Saturday 11th

Venus and Pluto meet up today. This influence can produce a seductive, intimate time or power struggles. You must make sure that you have agreed boundaries in place with a lover. It is possible that you can both drift too far away into a fantasy land with unhealthy habits such as alcohol. Stay safe.

Sunday 12th

There may be issues beyond your control within friendship groups today. You are outgoing and high spirited, but this may clash with others. Venus and Pluto are still together; they have the power to make great changes or endings together. A love connection can be transformed now.

Monday 13th

Mercury enters your intimacy sector now. Your ruler will help you have conversations that can sometimes be difficult or even taboo. Do not jump in too deep, take baby steps. Mars enters your relationship sector; prepare for a super sexy time or an exhausting one. Use his energy wisely.

Tuesday 14th

The Moon slips into your hidden sector today. Get confident about sharing your deepest self with another. You can have a low image of yourself and feel you are unworthy. Do not hide away; you are allowed to enjoy the little luxuries of life out in the open, too.

Wednesday 15th

Why do you feel guilty? You are too hard on yourself right now. The Moon meets Uranus and you feel this like an intrusion into your private life. Saturn is making it more difficult for you as he is reminding you of how far is too far. Pull back if you need to.

Thursday 16th

The Moon's connection to Venus and Pluto can make you uneasy if you let it. It is best that you recognise this energy of deep change in your hidden and intimate sectors as a need to be more open in relationships. Try to feel more and analyse less.

Friday 17th

You feel more like yourself, as the Moon hits familiar ground in your sector of self. In your own sign, you are more confident and outgoing. Reach out to the future and envisage a new you. Your inner compass is guiding you. There is high activity in your love life today.

Saturday 18th

Venus turns retrograde now in your intimacy sector. You may become reserved and turn your back on a loved one. You may also find it difficult to focus on the steps you need to climb that mountain to success. Expect endings or the return of a lost love during this time.

Sunday 19th

As the festive season looms closer, a Full Moon in your own sign highlights all that you have been through this year. This is the perfect time to evaluate your journey so far. Celebrate your successes, mourn your losses and do not look back with regret.

Monday 20th

You may feel the need to stay in your own home today. The coming weeks can be exhausting, so use this time to get comfortable in your own space. Treat yourself to favourite foods and get your tribe around. You may have a heart versus head battle today, but this should be brief.

Tuesday 21st

The Winter Solstice arrives, and the longest night asks that you pause, reflect and still your mind. You may see some conflict between men and women in the family. Review your role as a responsible nurturer and think about those who nourish you. Give thanks for family love today.

Wednesday 22nd

Today you will probably be actively catching up with people. Perhaps the parties have already started. Phone calls, messages and short trips are likely. Be careful that you do not get drawn into an argument with a person from your social sector. Make sure all jobs are done today.

Thursday 23rd

Jupiter has returned to the final degree of your travel sector. He wants you to get out and explore the wider world but is asking you to make sure that there is nothing you have overlooked. Your inquisitive mind will be able to spot if there is something you need to attend to now.

Friday 24th

The Moon moves into your family sector just as the celebrations begin. There is touchy energy from the planets, suggesting that there will be a lot of people vying to take control of the festive activities. Stay away from the chaos, or use your gifts of communication to bring peace.

Saturday 25th

Venus has retrograded to meet Pluto once more. This can be awkward on a day where people have joined together to celebrate. Power and control can be an issue today. Mercury and Uranus bring lively chatter and surprises but there is a chance that it will be less than ideal.

Sunday 26th

Today is less frenzied and you are able to find peace and balance. You may be called upon to mediate or host the entertainment. The Moon makes a nice connection to Venus and Pluto, suggesting that loving transformations can be achieved if they are worked at.

Monday 27th

Spend today alone or with a special person. Your creative sector is highlighted with good, assertive energy and responsibility. Maybe a clean-up is needed. Set the pace for the day and restore harmony to your home or your love relationships. Quality time alone will also help you quieten your mind today.

Tuesday 28th

Just as you thought it was all over, the planetary energy throws more tension at you. Venus retrograde may see you bringing a permanent end to something you have been working on stealthily. Make sure that this is not a knee-jerk reaction; there is no coming back from this.

Wednesday 29th

Massive Jupiter enters your work sector now. This will be beneficial to you over the next year. He will bring luck and optimism and enlarge everything he touches, including your workload. As you are prone to dreaming in this area, he can expand those too, so be careful what you wish for now.

Thursday 30th

Mercury and Pluto meet in your intimacy sector. You will find that your conversations become deeper and take on a darker edge. You are in a place where the mysteries of life are interesting you more than ever. Choose your teachers in this area wisely.

Friday 31st

The year ends with the Moon meeting the point of past actions. This is a great time to reflect on what karma you decide to leave behind you as the year ends. Emotions and actions will be high today in your relationships. Think back to what 2021 has taught you.

Gemini

·················

PEOPLE WHO SHARE
YOUR SIGN

PEOPLE WHO
SHARE YOUR SIGN

· · · · · · · · · · · · · · · · ·

The voices of Geminians are loud, clear and capable of moving
mountains. Their influential and contagious words often
have a global impact, whether it's a Tweet from U.S. President
Donald Trump or a song from Bob Dylan. Discover the
articulate Geminians who share your exact birthday and see if
you can spot the similarities.

22nd May

Novak Djokovic (1987), Arturo Vidal (1987), Maggie Q (1979),
Ginnifer Goodwin (1978), Naomi Campbell (1970), Steven
Morrissey (1959), George Best (1946), Laurence Olivier (1907),
Arthur Conan Doyle (1859)

23rd May

Ryan Coogler (1986), Richard Ayoade (1977), Manuela
Schwesig (1974), George Osborne (1971), Melissa McBride
(1965), Drew Carey (1958), Marvelous Marvin Hagler (1954),
Joan Collins (1933), Rosemary Clooney (1928)

24th May

Joey Logano (1990), G-Eazy (1989), Dermot O'Leary (1973), Eric
Cantona (1966), Rajdeep Sardesai (1965), Kristin Scott Thomas
(1960), Priscilla Presley (1945), Patti LaBelle (1944), Bob
Dylan (1941), Queen Victoria of the United Kingdom (1819)

25th May

Brec Bassinger (1999), Aly Raisman (1994), Roman Reigns (1985),
Rasheeda (1982), Joe King (1980), Cillian Murphy (1976),
Mike Myers (1963), Paul Weller (1958), Ian McKellen (1939)

26th May

Juan Cuadrado (1988), Scott Disick (1983), Lauryn Hill (1975),
Helena Bonham Carter (1966), Lenny Kravitz (1964), Jeremy
Corbyn (1949), Stevie Nicks (1948), John Wayne (1907)

27th May

Lily-Rose Depp (1999), André 3000 (1975), Jamie Oliver
(1975), Paul Bettany (1971), Joseph Fiennes (1970), Paul
Gascoigne (1967), Heston Blumenthal (1966), Henry Kissinger
(1923), Christopher Lee (1922)

28th May

Cameron Boyce (1999), John Stones (1994), Carey Mulligan
(1985), Jake Johnson (1978), Kylie Minogue (1968), John
Fogerty (1945), Gladys Knight (1944)

29th May

Maika Monroe (1993), Riley Keough (1989), Melanie B (1975),
Laverne Cox (1972), Noel Gallagher (1967), Carol Kirkwood
(1962), La Toya Jackson (1956), Rebbie Jackson (1950), John F.
Kennedy, U.S. President (1917)

30th May

Sean Giambrone (1999), Jake Short (1997), Jennifer Ellison (1983), Steven Gerrard (1980), Remy Ma (1980), Idina Menzel (1971), Mark Sheppard (1964)

31st May

Normani (1996), Azealia Banks (1991), Reggie Yates (1983), Colin Farrell (1976), Archie Panjabi (1972), Brooke Shields (1965), Viktor Orbán (1963), Lea Thompson (1961), Clint Eastwood (1930), Walt Whitman (1819)

1st June

Tom Holland (1996), Amy Schumer (1981), Alanis Morissette (1974), Heidi Klum (1973), Ronnie Wood (1947), Morgan Freeman (1937), Marilyn Monroe (1926)

2nd June

Sergio Agüero (1988), Morena Baccarin (1979), Dominic Cooper (1978), Justin Long (1978), Zachary Quinto (1977), A.J. Styles (1977), Wentworth Miller (1972), Andy Cohen (1968), Jeanine Pirro (1951), Charlie Watts (1941)

3rd June

Mario Götze (1992), Imogen Poots (1989), Michelle Keegan (1987), Rafael Nadal (1986), Anderson Cooper (1967), James Purefoy (1964), Susannah Constantine (1962), Allen Ginsberg (1926), Tony Curtis (1925), M. Karunanidhi (1924), King George V of the United Kingdom (1865)

4th June

Mackenzie Ziegler (2004), Lucky Blue Smith (1998), Brandon Jenner (1981), T.J. Miller (1981), Russell Brand (1975), Angelina Jolie (1975), Izabella Scorupco (1970)

5th June

Troye Sivan (1995), Amanda Crew (1986), Pete Wentz (1979), Nick Kroll (1978), Mark Wahlberg (1971), Ron Livingston (1967), Rick Riordan (1964), Kathleen Kennedy (1953), Ken Follett (1949)

6th June

Ryan Higa (1990), Natalie Morales-Rhodes (1972), Paul Giamatti (1967), Jason Isaacs (1963), Colin Quinn (1959), Björn Borg (1956), Sukarno, Indonesian President (1901), Thomas Mann (1875)

7th June

George Ezra (1993), Emily Ratajkowski (1991), Iggy Azalea (1990), Michael Cera (1988), Anna Kournikova (1981), Bill Hader (1978), Bear Grylls (1974), Prince (1958), Liam Neeson (1952), Tom Jones (1940)

8th June

Rosanna Pansino (1985), Javier Mascherano (1984), Kanye West (1977), Shilpa Shetty (1975), Julianna Margulies (1966), Tim Berners-Lee (1955), Bonnie Tyler (1951), Nancy Sinatra (1940), Joan Rivers (1933), Jerry Stiller (1927), Barbara Bush (1925)

9th June

Tanya Burr (1989), Mae Whitman (1988), Natalie Portman (1981), Matt Bellamy (1978), Miroslav Klose (1978), Johnny Depp (1963), Michael J. Fox (1961), Aaron Sorkin (1961)

10th June

Kate Upton (1992), Faith Evans (1973), Bill Burr (1968), Elizabeth Hurley (1965), Jeanne Tripplehorn (1963), Carlo Ancelotti (1959), Judy Garland (1922), Prince Philip, Duke of Edinburgh (1921)

11th June

Kodak Black (1997), Claire Holt (1988), Shia LaBeouf (1986), Joshua Jackson (1978), Peter Dinklage (1969), Hugh Laurie (1959), Gene Wilder (1933), Jacques Cousteau (1910)

12th June

Philippe Coutinho (1992), Dave Franco (1985), Kendra Wilkinson (1985), Adriana Lima (1981), Lil Duval (1977), Anne Frank (1929), George H. W. Bush, U.S. President (1924)

13th June

Aaron Taylor-Johnson (1990), Kat Dennings (1986), Mary-Kate and Ashley Olsen (1986), DJ Snake (1986), Chris Evans (1981), Steve-O (1974), Tim Allen (1953), Stellan Skarsgård (1951), W. B. Yeats (1865)

14th June

Jesy Nelson (1991), Lucy Hale (1989), Torrance Coombs (1983), Alan Carr (1976), Steffi Graf (1969), Boy George (1961), Donald Trump, U.S. President (1946), Che Guevara (1928)

15th June

Mohamed Salah (1992), Neil Patrick Harris (1973), Leah Remini (1970), Ice Cube (1969), Courteney Cox (1964), Helen Hunt (1963), Xi Jinping, General Secretary of the Communist Party of China (1953), Erik Erikson (1902)

16th June

John Newman (1990), Fernando Muslera (1986), Daniel Brühl (1978), Eddie Cibrian (1973), John Cho (1972), Tupac Shakur (1971), Jürgen Klopp (1967), Stan Laurel (1890), Geronimo (1829)

17th June

Kendrick Lamar (1987), Marie Avgeropoulos (1986), Venus Williams (1980), Sven Nys (1976), Tory Burch (1966), Greg Kinnear (1963), Barry Manilow (1943), M. C. Escher (1898), Igor Stravinsky (1882)

18th June

Willa Holland (1991), Pierre-Emerick Aubameyang (1989), Josh Dun (1988), Richard Madden (1986), Blake Shelton (1976), Isabella Rossellini (1952), Paul McCartney (1942), Delia Smith (1941), Barack Obama Sr. (1936)

19th June

KSI (1993), Macklemore (1983), Aidan Turner (1983), Zoe Saldana (1978), Boris Johnson (1964), Laura Ingraham (1963), Paula Abdul (1962), Salman Rushdie (1947)

20th June

Christopher Mintz-Plasse (1989), Mike Birbiglia (1978), Quinton Jackson (1978), Frank Lampard (1978), Roy Nelson (1976), Mateusz Morawiecki, Polish Prime Minister (1968), Nicole Kidman (1967), John Goodman (1952), Lionel Richie (1949), Brian Wilson (1942)

21st June

Lana Del Rey (1985), Prince William, Duke of Cambridge (1982), Brandon Flowers (1981), Chris Pratt (1979), Juliette Lewis (1973), Joko Widodo, Indonesian President (1961), Michel Platini (1955), Benazir Bhutto, Pakistani Prime Minister (1953)